Human Capital Analytics

How to Harness the Potential of Your Organization's Greatest Asset

Gene Pease
Boyce Byerly
Jac Fitz-enz

WILEY

John Wiley & Sons, Inc.

Library of Congress Cataloging-in-Publication Data

Pease, Gene, 1950–
    Human capital analytics : how to harness the potential of your organization's
greatest asset / Gene Pease, Boyce Byerly, Jac Fitz-enz.
        p. cm. — (Wiley & SAS business series)
    Includes index.
    ISBN 978-1-118-46676-6 (cloth) — ISBN 978-1-118-50697-4 (ePDF) —
    ISBN 978-1-118-50698-1 (Mobi) — ISBN 978-1-118-50699-8 (ePub)
        1. Human capital.   2. Personnel management.   I. Byerly, Boyce, 1962–
    II. Fitz-enz, Jac.   III. Title.
    HD4904.7.P362 2013
    658.3′01—dc23

                                                              2012030212

Printed in the United States of America

10 9 8 7 6 5 4

*I want to thank my parents for their lifelong love and for teaching
me the value of sticking to it, in spite of the obstacles; my
incredible wife, Pamela, and daughters, Tiffany and Heather,
who inspire me daily; and my sister, Susan, and brothers,
Jeff and Scott, for their constant support. My longtime buddies
Manny, Dennis, and Jeff, thank you for your friendship.*

—Gene Pease

■ ■ ■

*I'd like to thank my family for giving what I needed to do this all
in the first place: my parents, who taught me the value of
hard work and perseverance; my sisters, Marilynn, who led the
way in turning dreams into books, and Joni, who has always
been a pillar of support; and my sons, Cameron, Blake, and
Alexei, who inspire me, bring out the best in me, and give me
a reason to do big things.*

—Boyce Byerly

■ ■ ■

*I thank the many people who had the foresight and courage
to support me along the trail. Without their encouragement
I probably would have given up the quest. Most important to
me was Bob Coon, my best friend and golf buddy. We worked
together on measurement at Four-Phase Systems in the late
1970s, and later he followed me and became president of
Saratoga Institute. Thanks, Robert.*

—Jac Fitz-enz

Contents

Preface

The value proposition that an enterprise has created has shifted. The value of a modern company is in the intangibles, most of which are human capital of one form or another: expertise, customer relationships, employer brand, intellectual property, and business processes. The companies that will thrive and prosper are those that get the most out of their human capital, and that requires they understand what is going on with their workforce, how investments affect it, and how to communicate those changes effectively with all parts of the enterprise. The human resources industry is just beginning to grasp the value of understanding its human capital and evolving from a shepherd's role to one that can bring change and add significant strategic value.

There has been quite a bit written recently about big data and the power of analytics. Yet not much has been written on predictive analytics and even less on human capital predictive analytics. Rigorous analysis that provides true impact and shows organizations how to optimize their human capital investments through predictive analytics is necessary for organizations to outperform their competitors in today's competitive environment.

Building on the work of Jac and his HCM:21 model (Human Capital Metrics for the 21st Century) and applying advanced statistical methodology, coupled with today's computing power, we felt the need to write a book that showed how to accomplish the holy grail of human capital analysis: predictive analytics. The book starts with an overview of human capital analytics and then imparts the major lessons we have learned from many years doing this work. The early chapters focus on how to get organized, with subjects such as alignment and a measurement plan and the organization of data sources. The middle discusses metrics in organizations, how they are organized, and what is useful in dashboards, descriptive statistics, and correlations. The last chapters highlight what we call optimization, how to get beyond business impact and ROI to predictive analytics, and how to present the findings to effect organizational change. Each chapter is accompanied by a case study from a world-leading company that illustrates the chapter topic to show how our lessons are applied in complicated environments.

We hope this book will be read by both the leaders of human resources, as well as their associates outside of HR. We believe it will inspire you to apply the same tools used to evaluate and improve finance, marketing, and operations investments with the same rigor to human capital investments. We also hope to show HR practitioners that the lessons learned in this book and lots of hard work will result in their achieving significant improvement in their deployment of human capital investments and will ultimately drive organizational strategic goals.

Acknowledgments

The work that is represented in this book is the result of tireless collaboration for seven years of an amazing team at Capital Analytics and decades of Dr. Jac's work. It was a long time in coming, and a lot of people helped along the way. We would not be here today without the support of the Capital Analytics investors: Phil Buchanan, PhD; Barrie Trinkle; Joan Troy Ontjes, PhD; Dr. Andy Collins and Joey Colclough; and later on Reed Clevenger, Chris Hens, and Mike Wood. Thank you to our advisory board members, whose wisdom has helped us immensely: Sandy Costa; Steve Bistritz, PhD; Karen Jackson; Julia Gometz; Harold Stolovitch, PhD; Dean Spitzer, PhD; Diane Paces-Wiles; David Vance, PhD; and Hugh Wrigley.

After we put together the company with the help of the investors, we needed someone who completely understood the mind of the client. Bonnie Beresford was our client on the Chrysler projects and pushed us harder and drove us to better work than any client ever had. When we were ready to expand, she was the perfect choice to lead our client engagements and continues to be the person who understands how to realize value for the clients more than anyone else. (We were kind of hoping that once we hired her, she wouldn't work us quite as hard, but alas, we should have seen that one coming.) The team that has joined us at Capital is really our dream team, and we would not trade them for anybody. Melissa Lewis; Lori Ches; Jenny Murnane, PhD; and John Zonneveld have contributed brilliantly, with tireless late nights, passion, and creativity.

Before Capital Analytics, Boyce collaborated with David Hadden around the problem of measuring the return on investment on corporate training as merely a peripheral aspect of a skill gap analysis and management software tool. That "peripheral aspect" has spun into the current work on the broader topic of measurement of human capital. A lot of people contributed to that development. Eliot Cramer at UNC knew how general linear models *worked*, all the way down to the nuts and bolts. Victor Lewis and Craig Anderson built an elegant early solution in software. Cami Kinahan helped us understand how to build a relationship with a client. Michael Chevalier put in long hours as a first-rate researcher. Karie Willyerd was one of our greatest and earliest evangelists while at Sun and served on our first advisory board. Susan Knox and Roland Smith contributed to the relationships and business savvy that helped turn a dream into a reality.

We would also like to acknowledge and thank our continued strategic partnership with Bellevue University, Bellevue University's Human Capital Lab, and its PhD program: specifically, President Mary Hawkins, PhD; Executive Vice President Michael Echols, PhD; and PhD Program Manager Jennifer Moss, PhD. Mike's vision and tenacity have transformed Bellevue into a world-class thought leader on human capital optimization.

We want to thank the clients who have trusted us to go inside the deepest recesses of their companies and shared their stories, their missions, and their data with us and let us be a part of it. Without them, we couldn't have developed the methodology that forms this book. The professional community in our field, especially the members of ISPI, could have felt like competitors but chose to be colleagues, advisers, and inspirations instead. We wish to thank the executives at each of our case study companies for allowing us to share their stories: Cedric T. Coco and Carmen Neudorff of Lowe's; Dr. Fiona Jamison and Dr. Heather Black of Spring International; Hogo Bague, Bob Farrell, and Mike Sokol of Rio Tinto; Mary Morand and Debbie Mandell of U.S. Bank; Mark Engelsdorfer and Fred DePerez of Chrysler; Ron Lawrence and Ruth Kennedy of VF; and Lucy Dinwiddie (now at GE) and John Hine of ConAgra Foods.

The crunch that went into writing the book in 2012 required a lot of labor. We especially want to thank Sara Jensen and Mia Heckendorf for their editing and keeping the authors on schedule, as well as Olivia Parr-Rud for her assistance with the final internal edit. In addition, we wish to thank our editor at John Wiley & Sons, Sheck Cho, for being such a pleasure to work with. We want to thank the Wiley editorial team, particularly Stacey Rivera, who reviewed every chapter and offered substantial feedback.

And thank you, SAS Institute, for supporting this project.

Introduction

Realizing the Dream: From Nuisance to Necessity

P ersonnel and Training are in the annex. We put them where they can't hurt anyone."

That was the direction I received on a beautiful September morning in 1969 when I walked into the headquarters of Wells Fargo Bank in San Francisco. I arrived for my new position in the training department. Naturally, I went to the great granite edifice that housed the main branch and many floors of offices at 464 California Street. Much to my surprise, I was directed to the annex four blocks away. As I walked two blocks east and two blocks north, I wondered, "Why am I going to the annex when most of my customers, managers, and employees are in the main building?"

This stunning experience started me dreaming. It eventually brought me to the work of Gene Pease and Boyce Byerly, the coauthors of this book. About 10 years ago, Boyce initiated the groundwork to develop the methodology and analytical tools that form the core intellectual assets of Capital Analytics today. The work began with applying statistical analysis to training investments. It drifted into HR, as clients began to request the application of predictive analytics to increasingly complex investments. A few years later, I learned about Boyce's business partner Gene and their work at Capital Analytics, where they were applying statistical analysis to a broad range of human capital issues. Eventually, I invited Gene to speak at the Human Capital Metrics conference I run each year for the Conference Board. Gene and I decided that our approaches were complementary and agreed to coauthor this book with Boyce.

STARTING FROM THE BACK ROW

Prior to the Wells Fargo job, my career had been mostly in line jobs and sales. These were highly valued functions. Now I was about to join a unit that clearly was held in low regard within the bank. It didn't take very long for me to learn why this was the case.

Bankers live on numbers. They count success in quantitative terms, such as revenue and profits, while monitoring and recording it in instruments such as income statements and balance sheets. In 1969, these were foreign concepts for the personnel and training (P&T) folks. They liked people. The only counting they did was how many people the bank employed. The thoughts of cost or value were disregarded in favor of concerns about employee satisfaction. In my mind, the P&T people just wanted bank employees to be happy. The bank's management wanted employees to be happy, too—but more important, they wanted them to be contributing value that could be counted objectively and quantitatively.

THE VALUE DREAM

As strange as P&T's attitude seems now, it was not that unusual in 1969. At that time, most people in those functions across industries and indeed across countries shared the same happiness mentality. I was working on my master's degree at night in the early 1970s. One assignment was to design a job description for a job that did not exist at that time. Based on my experience at Wells and with other personnel types, I designed a job titled "Organizational Hugger." Its primary purpose was to make employees happy.

Fortunately, in the 1960s and1970s there were some dreamers who hoped for the day when the stigma of P&T would be replaced by an appreciation for the business value that the function contributed. A couple of brave but obscure proponents of the value dream started to publish isolated case studies of value added though training. Way back in 1954, Don Kirkpatrick wrote his doctoral dissertation on evaluating employee relations programs. In the 1960s, his dissertation found its way into the *ASTD Journal* and spawned his now famous "Four Levels of Evaluation." Conversely, this was followed by a speaker at ASTD's national training conference who stated emphatically that the value of training could not be determined.

After a year of struggling with my colleagues at Wells Fargo, I wrote a piece for the *Personnel Journal* titled "The Measurement Imperative."[1] Published in 1971, this was the first of more than 350 articles and a dozen books I've authored around this topic. In 1976, Ray Killian of Belk Department Stores published the groundbreaking *Human Resources: An ROI Approach.*[2] Its message fell on deaf ears. At about the same time Jack Phillips, later the founder of the ROI Institute, wrote his first of a steady stream of articles and books on training evaluation.

In 1980, after Motorola bought the computer company where I was head of HR, I decided it was time to commit myself totally to the dream. Accordingly, I founded Saratoga Institute and began researching and providing training on the human resources metrics we had developed in the computer company. Initially, the approach was mostly defensive. We had to show that HR was not an expense unit. It was a function that had the potential to add value on both sides of the income statement: revenue growth and expense reduction. We developed a set of metrics that HR people could use to communicate. In the late 1980s, when we launched the benchmark Human Resources Effectiveness Reports, the Society of Human Resource Management (SHRM) provided some initial funding. However, SHRM refused to recommend these metrics as the standard. Almost 30 years later, SHRM organized an effort to establish standard metrics. Interestingly, many of these metrics were derivatives of the 1980s program.

For a long time, no other thought leaders emerged. Then, in the 1990s, Mark Huselid began publishing annual survey data that established the links between human resources investments and company productivity. Shortly thereafter, John Boudreau began writing on the connections between people and business results. Around 2006, Laurie Bassi began publishing her research on the connection of human capital investments to financial returns and stock prices. Most recently, Davenport and Harris's books on analytics have captured the attention of many in human resources. Now, we have reached a point where every issue of human resource and training magazines carries pieces on analytics. Finally, it seems that human capital analytics is crossing the threshold and gaining credibility within human resources department operations.

BARRIERS IN THE HUMAN RESOURCE AREA

Early attempts to promote the analytics dream stirred imaginations but garnered little commitment. Instead, we encountered a mixture of apathy and hostility. The strong prevailing attitude was that people should simply be accepted as valuable and no attempt should be made to apply numbers to their performance. Some said it would dehumanize them. Unfortunately, accounting systems have always treated employee investments as expenses. Absent a countering systemic view, employees will continue to be relegated to the expense column on the income statement, rather than a valuable asset on the balance sheet.

ORGANIZATIONS ARE ALL ABOUT PEOPLE, NOT THINGS

Organizations are composed of things owned or rented, such as equipment, material, money, and facilities. Organizations also consist of things that are not owned or rented, their people. Of the two groups, only one is active—the people. All other variables are passive and inert. Without people, all of those assets do little more than depreciate. Even cash, if not invested through some human act, will depreciate in value through inexorable inflation. The finest computer, vehicle, building, codified process, or pile of inventory cannot add value without human application. Still, management persists in spending millions to acquire things such as new computers but refuses to invest in the training of employees to leverage the computer's capabilities.

Consider the example of one of my sons, who worked in a major retailer. At one point, the company invested in new cash register software. After installation, when the salesclerks asked how to run the software, they were told bluntly, "Read the manual." The end result was many errors, impatient customers, and lost sales until, through multiple trials, the clerks learned the system. During the course of this period of frustration and error, the frustrated clerks rang up any sales figure they could get (always less than the tag price) just to finish the transaction.

MANAGING RISK

The market is a cauldron of risk. Competition, government regulations, customers, technology, and employees are all high-risk issues today. Change is so rapid and radical that management is like a lottery. Managers place their bets and hope they made the right decision. Exacerbating that is the fact that managers are human. We are all flawed, no matter what our level of education or experience. In fact, without insight and objectively obtained data, experience can be a powerful enemy. What people have learned on the way up is often obsolete. The pressure to perform forces people to make decisions based on yesterday's events. Yet as powerful as they may have been, those past occurrences are not necessarily applicable to tomorrow's investment choices. This is precisely why we need analytics. Being bias free, analytic methods override human error in uncovering the hidden truths about a situation.

Descriptive, predictive, and prescriptive analytics allow us to do what I labeled "Manage tomorrow, today." Looking back descriptively through return on investment evaluations, we can learn why something happened the way it did. We can stop blaming people who can't defend themselves, which we do when we can't otherwise explain why things happen. After description, predictive analysis can show us a path that substantially raises the probability of future success. Prescriptive analysis shows us how to be successful tomorrow. The

likelihood of success increases through consistent, error-free performance supported by solid analytic methodology.

HISTORIC FUNDAMENTALS

Basically, there are five ways to quantify something: cost, time, quantity, quality, and human reaction. In management, we measure how
something changes over time and as the result of different activities.
However, we rarely measure how something is changing. Revenue,
expense, customers, and employees all move constantly. The fundamental questions are how much has each factor moved, in which
direction did it move, and was that direction desirable or undesirable?

In the 1970s, at the beginning of human resources measurement,
we monitored transactions. What did it cost to hire, train, pay, and
retain employees? How many did we hire, train, or retain? In time, the
question emerged: what matters? It became clear that even for a
background function such as HR, change should be viewed in terms of
its effect on the organization's goals. Gradually, we moved toward
performance monitoring. If we changed our hiring strategy, could
we see improvement in employee performance and attrition? If we
offered training, did we see productivity increase and rework
decrease? After showing this information to management, managers'
question was, "How do we compare?" So we began benchmarking,
which gained some popularity in the mid-1980s.

At Saratoga Institute, in 1985 we published the first national
benchmarks. They grew to eventually cover about 500 companies in
more than a dozen industries and 1,000 more in Asia Pacific, South
America, and Europe. Soon we began to see trends within industries
or regions. This was the first simple descriptive analysis. The new
question emerged, "Why was there a trend?" Through observation, we
speculated about the reasons, yet we had little proof. It wasn't until
the application of predictive analysis that we could make definitive
statements and back them up with objective data.

I left Saratoga Institute in 2002 in search of new ways of describing
human capital's effects. From 2006 through 2008, I published *The
Workforce Intelligence Report*, which was a best practices document
drawing on research across 700 companies. As I labored to collect the

data, I asked myself the question made popular by that 1969 Peggy Lee Grammy-winning song, "Is That All There Is?" I wondered whether we had we hit the end of the road in people analysis. Should we do what Peggy suggested—"break out the booze and have a ball—if that's all there is"?

INTANGIBLES

In 2001, Baruch Lev, professor of accounting at New York University, published his work on accounting for intangibles.[3] He defined intangibles assets as *"a claim to future benefits that does not have a physical or financial embodiment."*[4] (Italics added.)

Lev made a strong case for recognizing the value of intangibles on the balance sheet. He pointed out that for every $6 of market value of the Standard and Poor's 500 companies, only $1 appears on their balance sheets.

He admitted that these assets are high risk, lack control over their benefits, and lack markets.

Nevertheless, he argued that globalization and information technology have changed the structure of corporations and pushed intangibles into the role of the major value drivers of businesses in developed economies. Two of the three intangible value classes are organizational practices and human resources.

Shortly after the publication of *Intangibles*, I had the opportunity to visit Baruch Lev in his office at NYU. He told me that when he talked to financial executives, the interest level was quite high. Yet the action level remained quite low. Apparently, the prevailing belief is if something cannot be sold during a bankruptcy action (i.e., Kodak selling its patents), then it is not an asset. Clearly, it is time for accounting to open up to seeing the world as it really is, not as it was during the industrial era.

PREDICTABILITY

As recently as 2006, predictive analytics had not yet appeared in human resources. Yet it seemed to me that we needed a way to look into the future of human capital investments. We knew a lot about human resources practices and human capital outcomes and values, but we still could not forecast or predict the results of investments in people with any certainty. Predictive statistics were available and were being used in other functions, but I knew from decades of experience with HR practitioners that if we just pushed them into the statistical pool, they would drown. No one ever joined HR because he or she loved numbers. In fact, in many cases it was just the opposite. People wanted a job without numbers, just lots of hugging.

NEED FOR DEFINITION

No one whom I knew had a definitive idea of how to apply predictive analytics to human resources in a systematic way. Even SAS Institute, a leading analytics firm that I had consulted for in the late 1990s, had not made a strong commitment to analyzing HR. So we were left with the apocryphal question of Wilbur Wright, "It's a great theory, Orville, but will it fly?"

Just like the Wright brothers, we needed a vehicle to support our attempts to fly. I decided to enlist the support of some of the best brains in and around the human capital arena. Eventually, I obtained the backing of a dozen major firms and several thought leaders to build a predictive model. Particularly helpful were the thoughts of author Doug Hubbard and Professor Nick Bontis.

For 18 months, we labored to develop an interrogative model.[5] We needed a way to penetrate the obvious. The more we looked at it, the more I could see that analytics was split into two paths. Unlike what we thought in the beginning, statistical procedures are not the starting point. We needed to find out what we didn't know about any situation into which we wanted to apply statistical analysis before we threw metrics at it. In the end, we designed what is now known as HCM:21 (Human Capital Metrics the 21st Century).

BREAKTHROUGH

Partly through the acceptance of HCM:21 and the work of other thought leaders such as Gene Pease and Boyce Byerly, the dream has become a reality. HR practitioners have begun to embrace analytics, and organizational leaders are demanding increasing accountability from HR.

Analytics is the science of analysis. Analysis comes from the Greek, *analutika*, meaning "to separate the whole into its component parts." As I mentioned earlier, there are two levels of analytics. Descriptive analytics tells what has happened in the past and usually the cause of the outcome. Predictive analytics focuses on the future, telling what is likely to happen given a stated approach. Then prescriptive analytics tells us what to do to make it happen.

Predictive analytics is used in actuarial and financial services, insurance, telecommunications, retail, travel, health care, and pharmaceuticals, among others. Internally, R&D, marketing, advertising, and customer service functions have been applying analytics to their work for many years. The irony is that while HR people have stubbornly claimed one could not predict the behavior of employees in a closed environment, those other functions have been analyzing and predicting customer behavior across the much more complex open marketplace.

Analytics promises to describe, with a high degree of probability, the behavior of people inside organizations. Now we are able to apply descriptive analytics to understand current human capital problems and prescriptive analytics to improve future outcomes from human capital investments.

PRACTICALITY

Businesspeople are driven to produce. This need is aggravated by the fact that there is seldom complete data around a complex situation. As a result, many managers race to a solution without fully understanding the surrounding circumstances. In almost every client meeting, one of the first questions is, "What should we measure?" Yet in practice, measurement is the last step in analysis and planning.

Many analytics projects that I have encountered are one-off exercises to solve a single problem. In time, the project is completed with some degree of success. However, soon another problem or opportunity arises, and the discovery process starts from step one all over again. I find this very inefficient and often ineffective. I strongly believe, based on witnessing several poor-performing projects, that a well-defined, consistent, programmatic approach is necessary. In short, without an analytic model, managers are condemned to trial and error as they struggle to relearn an investigative process every time.

ANALYTICS MODEL FOUNDATION

Human capital management and analytics rest on two pillars. One is a logical framework of questions. The initial step is the development of the logic process. One of the books that had made the greatest impression on me in college was *Plato's Republic*, specifically the section where Socrates and Thrasymachus discuss "What Is Justice?" The questioning method impressed me as a great pathway into the application of predictive analysis. It asks penetrating questions to test beliefs and impressions, such as:

- What is happening?
- Why is it happening?
- What effect is it having on our organization?

Next, what is happening within our organization that is affecting our ability to perform or to reach new goals?

Then, given our knowledge of the marketplace and our organization,

- What options do we have to improve our position?

Those and several other probing questions test the logic of our position. In the end, they add confidence that we are starting along the right path.

The second supporting column is a combination of statistical analysis and computer technology that helps us analyze the qualitative and quantitative data we have in order to produce the most efficient, effective, and sustainable outcome.

Thus, the starting point is to understand the marketplace, as mentioned earlier, and then to assess our organization's strengths and weaknesses as they relate to market forces and to our systems, culture, brand, processes, and goals. This book addresses the practical application of these two pillars.

AWAKENING

This sums up more than three decades of struggle to understand, describe, and evaluate the work of the HR function. Even more important, it has greatly improved our knowledge of the results of human capital investments. Ultimately, that is our goal—to invest more wisely in human capital for the good of the people, as well as for the benefits to the organization. The good news is that the human resources profession is waking up to the potential value of analysis, particularly predictive analytics. Each year in the program I run for the Conference Board on measurement, the quality of the presentations is improving. This is a confirmation that more companies are applying analytics. At a personal level, this is very gratifying for me and a confirmation that 30 years of evangelizing was not wasted.

The furtherance of the awakening or realization of the dream is the purpose and hope of this book. Analytics is a complex science. When we apply it to human behavior in organizational settings, it becomes even more complex. Yet the joy of analytics is that it opens one's eyes to a vast landscape of possibilities.

—JAC FITZ-ENZ

NOTES

1. Jac Fitz-enz, "The Measurement Imperative," *Personnel Journal* 19 (1971).
2. Ray Killian, *Human Resources: An ROI Approach* (New York: AMACOM, 1976).
3. Baruch Lev, *Intangibles* (Washington, DC: Brookings Institution, 2001), p. 5.
4. Ibid.
5. Douglas Hubbard, *How to Measure Anything: Finding the Value of Intangibles in Business*, 2nd ed. (Hoboken, NJ: John Wiley and Sons, 2007).

CHAPTER 1

Human Capital Analytics

"Information is the oil of the 21st century, and analytics is the combustion engine . . . . pursuing this strategically will create an unprecedented amount of information of enormous variety and complexity."

—Peter Sondergaard, senior vice president,
Gartner; quoted in the *Register*[1]

Human capital analytics can be approached in many different ways. Some organizations are very sophisticated at people measurements, while others are just beginning to think about starting the measurement journey. Investments in your people, your most important asset, can show financial returns to the organization, while also showing benefit to the employee through improved engagement and retention. Analytics on human capital investments is a very powerful way to improve those returns, on both the individual and the organizational level. This book focuses on *predictive analytics,* analytics that not only measures impact but also helps optimize and prescribe future investments. We hope that this book will improve your understanding of the power of optimizing your people investments. In the end, you will know not only how your HR investments are performing but how to improve them as they are deployed.

13

Predictive analytics is being successfully applied in the private, public, nonprofit, educational, and government arenas. Organizations that apply analytics to their human capital generally outperform their competitors. In a 2010 study of 179 large companies, those organizations adopting "data-driven decision making" achieved productivity gains that were 5 to 6 percent higher than those that did not.[2]

This work has been perfected in many industries and organizational areas during the last 30 years. Davenport shows many areas where advanced analytics are being applied. The financial services industry uses advanced analytics for credit scoring, fraud detection, and underwriting. The retail industry uses analytics for marketing promotions, inventory replenishment, and demand forecasting. Manufacturing organizations use analytics for supply chain optimization and warranty analysis. The hospitality industry uses analytics for pricing, customer loyalty, and yield management. The transportation industry uses analytics for scheduling, routing, and yield optimization. Drugs are tested and taken to market using advanced analytics. Recently, this tool is being applied to the world of HR investments.[3]

It is one thing to be able to show the benefit of a human capital investment by calculating the business impact and its return on investment (ROI). But to gain insight into where the investment is working and where it is not allows you to identify opportunities for improvement. Building on the work from those thought leaders discussed in the introduction, we will show you the methodology behind getting to an *isolated* business impact using your company's data, rather than relying on subjective opinions gathered through surveys.

Understanding how the investment is working, while isolating the impact from all of the other variables internal and external to the organization, is not the end in itself. There are many methodologies to estimate the business impact and ROI of an investment. We will show you the value of isolating the impact that allows you to evolve to optimization by segmentation (job title, tenure, department, location, business unit, region, and so on)—understanding where the investment is working and where it is not. Understanding where your HR investments are having an impact and where they are not allows you to predictively increase or decrease your investment in each area. Isolating investments from all of the other variables is not simple, but we know it is the best way to achieve optimization. Accurate, isolated, and precise impact provides optimization almost as a free benefit.

Generally, there are two types of HR investments: direct and indirect. A direct investment has a clear, or direct, line of sight to the business outcome you are trying to achieve. Sales readiness initiatives most often are trying to increase revenue, gross margin, or new accounts. Customer call center training strives to decrease average handling time, or the number of calls escalated to the supervisor. An indirect investment does not have a direct line of sight to the business outcome. What are the business outcomes for a leadership develop-ment program, a mentoring program, or a performance management system? The outcomes are not so obvious, thus indirect. Our meth-odology applies to both.

This book is not for those who want to merely justify your HR investments, but for those who want to improve them. Relying on average business impact is limiting and sometimes even misleading. Consider these scenarios:

- Suppose in a retail organization your "customer first" program was increasing overall same-store revenue, but it was not working in the Northeast. Would you adjust anything?

- If your leadership development initiative was successfully building the management pipeline, but you discovered it was working only for men, what would you do?

- What if your new on-boarding program showed an increase in initial performance, but the benefit disappeared after the first six months. Would it still be worthwhile?

- Suppose your new call center training program successfully increased sales, but also increased call handling time. What would you need to know in order to see if the training was responsible and whether the overall return was worthwhile?

If you could answer these questions, of course you would make changes to your program. This is the power of optimization. You no longer need to deploy programs using anecdotes and myths, but rather evidence.

This book has seven case studies that will show you how leading organizations are using the power of analytics to improve their HR investments. In this chapter's case study, Lowe's home improvement stores will illustrate how advanced analytics is used to link employee engagement with store performance. In Chapter 2, Rio Tinto, a leading international mining company, shows how it aligned a safety program to not only its employees but to more than 50,000 contractors as well. In Chapter 3, we will show you how Sun Microsystems (since acquired by Oracle) developed measurement plans for the introduction of a social learning platform. In Chapter 4, U.S. Bank comes to terms with locating and using complex data. In Chapter 5, both Chrysler and VF Corporation (the world's largest apparel company) show you how they organized their existing data to provide insights into their workforce. In Chapter 6, Chrysler isolates how much of the superior performance, shown by trainees, was due to the training itself. And in Chapter 7, ConAgra Foods and Chrysler use predicative analytics to optimize their human capital investments.

Although the case studies we highlight are from large public companies, the work we will show you in the book can be simplified for smaller organizations.

HUMAN CAPITAL ANALYTICS CONTINUUM

Let's begin with the human capital analytics continuum—a look at how organizations collect and report data. Exhibit 1.1 shows our view of human capital analytics. The continuum is based on what we have seen in our work, starting with simple, commonly used techniques. Viewing the continuum as a mountain, we suggest that similar to mountain climbing, things become more difficult but the view improves as you reach higher ground.

The ascent begins with anecdotes or storytelling. Brinkerhoff has done some of the best work in this area, describing a mixture of ethnography and positive psychology in "Success Case Methodology."[4] This well-thought-out interview has important applications in clinical psychology, anthropology, expert systems, and many other areas.

Scorecards and dashboards are other important areas. Scorecards, most notably "Balanced Scorecards," are a strategic performance

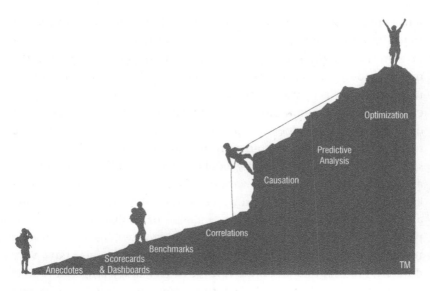

Exhibit 1.1 Continuum of Human Capital Analytics

management tool that can leverage automated surveys to track how an organization executes strategy and the consequences arising from business processes, most commonly referred to as activity metrics.[5] Scorecards characteristically have a mixture of financial and nonfinancial measures, each compared to its targets, all within a single concise report. They are an important step on the continuum, because this is where you must lay out the basic assumptions: what are your strategies, and what are the various ways in which you will measure them?

Dashboards share those characteristics. A dashboard is a distillation of the most important key performance indicators of a company that an executive can view at a glance. Dashboards might be an ad hoc effort put together on spreadsheets or even lower-tech tools, or they may involve special-purpose programming. Chapter 5, "What Dashboards Are Telling You: Descriptive Statistics and Correlations," details how basic descriptive statistics, such as those in dashboards, can be rich sources of data.

Benchmarks are another step on the continuum. Benchmarking has long been used as a standard tool; the idea is that studying the best-run companies in a specific area can be very beneficial in terms of setting things such as salary, training levels, desired turnover rates, and so forth. In our opinion, benchmarking needs to be taken with a grain of salt, perhaps several grains of salt. First, our experiences in understanding and acquiring corporate data have been humbling; understanding accurately the data within one company is quite enough of a job some days. Tying together data from a variety of different companies does not produce a feeling of confidence. Take turnover, for example. Within a given company, turnover data can be split into regrettable and nonregrettable turnover and further split into avoidable and nonavoidable varieties.[6] Our experience tells us that identifying the nature of the turnover is crucial to corporate strategy, and this information may not be available or similar between companies. Furthermore, companies are not always willing to accurately report their data, for all sorts of reasons. Organizations also have very different philosophies and practices. We have worked with call centers that hired carefully and treated their employees well by offering quality grooming and training; this philosophy resulted in expensive employees, but ones who stayed with the company and performed at a high level. Other call centers with whom we have worked hired unselectively, paid low wages, cracked the whip, and hosed down the decks when employees didn't perform. Which of the two philosophies is preferable depends on the business strategies of the organization. Finally, there's just something intrinsically contradictory to us about aspiring to greatness by doing the same thing that everyone else does.

Correlations and causations are the next two stages in the continuum. We use these phrases in a way that we find comfortable but may not entirely agree with standard usage. "Correlations" we use to describe the descriptive statistics that might occur on a sophisticated dashboard. Where are sales highest? Did the trained employees outperform the untrained ones? These are rich data mines for understanding business resources and human capital.

Causation is the next level beyond correlation. We would like to have a nickel for every time we have repeated the phrase "correlation does not imply causation" around our offices. We hope it will continue to be repeated, to junior business analysts and freshmen, until the Earth quits turning on its axis. Newspapers and books are full of correlations, tying together every conceivable item to support policy decisions. Umbrellas need to be banned because it ends up raining on days where everyone carries them. Ice cream sales and murder rates leap together in the dog days of summer. We like Cascio and Boudreau's three-part criteria of causation:[7]

1. Two events must show a clear and statistically significant connection,
2. One event must precede the other, and
3. All other plausible causes must be ruled out.

We view the final stage as optimization, the holy grail of HR measurement. Optimization is having the intelligence to understand where the impact is occurring. Optimization is intimately wrapped up with causation. Without understanding all of the factors that control impact, it is impossible to be sure that you have correctly assessed impact. The really positive side of having assessed and measured the different factors that control and mediate impact is that you can use them to control future impact and improve outcomes. If you have controlled and assessed the impact of the various factors, you are able to use them prescriptively. If you know how much tenure controls performance and how the various tenure levels benefit from training, the logical consequence is that you can now specify where training should be focused and what new programs need to be created for areas that do not show the benefits.

When we speak at industry events, we typically survey the audience on where its members are on this continuum. Based on our feedback, we believe most organizations are on the lower left of the continuum, obtaining information from their dashboards and scorecards. So, where is your organization on this human capital analytics continuum? This book will show you how to move up the continuum into the world of predictive analytics, enabling you to optimize your human capital investments.

There are, of course, other ways to talk about the continuum of human capital measurement. Several different measurement methodologies are particular to learning and development but have limitations when we apply advanced analytics to them. In developing our continuum, we are striving for a broader view of all human capital investments, independent of learning and development. We think a broader view is necessary for HR.

The application of predictive analytics allows you incredible insights into your workforce and enables you to improve your HR investments, both financially and for your employees. In our first case study, Lowe's will show you the power of this work.

CASE STUDY

CONNECTING PEOPLE INVESTMENTS AND BUSINESS OUTCOMES AT LOWE'S: USING VALUE LINKAGE ANALYTICS TO LINK EMPLOYEE ENGAGEMENT TO BUSINESS PERFORMANCE*

The ability to formulate and implement strategy is one of the most important *and elusive* enablers of sustained organizational success. Successful strategy execution requires that the purpose and priorities of the organization be defined and the strategy and tactics for achieving them be clearly aligned.

Aligning strategy and execution is a difficult task for most businesses. Research indicates that 70% to 90% of organizations fail to realize success from their strategies.[8] Human resource leaders, in particular, often find it difficult to strategically align and integrate their HR functional strategies, outputs, and measures to business priorities.

HR measures are typically cost-based, lagging metrics that either measure workforce-related expenditures (for example, headcount costs) or efficiencies in the HR function itself (such as position fill rates). Most HR executives lack forward-looking data that help drive business strategy. This puts the people agenda at a significant disadvantage when HR engages in strategy and execution discussions with other executives. Although there is general recognition that people truly are an organization's greatest asset, there seem to be limited ways to measure their activities effectively.

During the last 20 years, employee engagement has become generally accepted as one indicator of business performance. Applied correctly, engagement data can act as an early warning system for revenue and profits. The statistical relationship between engagement

*This case study was written by Cedric T. Coco, senior vice president, Learning & Organizational Effectiveness, Lowe's Companies, Inc.; Dr. Fiona Jamison, senior vice president, Research and Consulting, Spring International; and Dr. Heather Black, vice president, Research Analytics, Spring International. It was published in HRPS's journal *People & Strategy*.

and financial success has been shown in numerous studies. For example, in the report *Employee Engagement Underpins Business Transformation*, companies with highly engaged employees outperformed those with less-engaged employees in three key financial measures—operating income, net income growth, and earnings per share.[9]

However, there are two critical issues that are still keeping most organizations from measuring the actual financial impact of engagement on their bottom line. First, identifying the financial impact of engagement is, to date, mostly correlative—organizations know there is a connection but do not have sufficient cause-effect data necessary to make specific improvements for people or operational performance. Second, as a recent survey of HR leaders showed, companies that statistically test these relationships typically only examine relationships among different HR data points, rather than making linkages to non-HR data as well. In fact, only a handful of organizations link HR to financial or other non-HR data.[10]

In order to show how HR helps drive business strategy, the relationships of HR data point to other non-HR data metrics throughout the organization that must be measured. The statistical techniques must be sophisticated enough to show cause and effect, while managing the complexity of the organization's business processes.

Importance of Integrating Data

For many organizations, integrating HR, customer, operations, financial, and other types of data can be daunting. Barriers to conducting this type of analysis can range from simply not knowing all of the types of data the organization is currently collecting to dealing with incompatible or redundant systems housing the data, to data quality issues (information gaps) and issues in working across organizational silos.

In 2007, Lowe's began the journey to establish a data-driven, HR business model to show causal linkages from HR to business outcomes. Lowe's understood that employees are crucial to competitive advantage and could not accept that people were the largest single most unmeasured asset. Business leaders intuitively knew the relationships existed, but a proven decision model would help identify the people and HR priorities by showing which areas had the greatest business impact. Lowe's collaborated with an outside consultant to develop a systematic methodology for determining the impact of people on financial results.

Lowe's set out to create a value linkage decision model to define the causal linkages between people measures and key metrics, such as retail shrink (a retail metric related to inventory loss due to shoplifting, employee

(Continued)

theft, or supplier fraud), revenue, and customer satisfaction. Lowe's used the methodology to link HR data (engagement surveys, turnover data, sick time, and so forth) to marketing data (customer satisfaction, loyalty, value, and so on), operations data (inventory shrink, safety, and so forth) and financial metrics (sales per square foot, net income before tax, and so on).

Step 1: Establishing Buy-In

For Lowe's, the first step was to establish executive buy-in. Human resources is the steward for many people decisions, but Lowe's objectives went beyond making HR more efficient or effective. Lowe's wanted to make better people decisions for the organization, not just better HR decisions. Lowe's had already seen the impact of its engagement work, and the HR leadership team championed linkage analysis as an extension of this work.

Yet from the beginning, Lowe's had skeptics about its ability to create a viable model to show the impact of engagement on the bottom line. The Lowe's HR team recognized early on in the process that a cross-functional team was required to build and achieve support for a linkage model. A cross-functional team was created with an emphasis on finance, market research, and operations to help build the model.

Beyond building the cross-functional project team, HR's primary role in the model development was to facilitate the process. HR's larger role for organization alignment would come after the model was built.

Step 2: The Discovery Process

The second step was to conduct a data audit and evaluation process starting with the employee attitudinal data from Lowe's employee engagement results. Establishing quality metrics is essential before embarking on any linkage analysis approach. For example, organizations cannot assume that simply conducting an engagement survey provides sufficient data to conduct a linkage analysis. Many organizations collect only a sample survey each year, may use a limited response scale (less than a five-point scale), and may not identify results by location or group or even distinguish results by manager and nonmanager. These components have been found to be very important for linkage analysis.

After assessing the employee opinion data and other data traditionally collected by HR, the project team turned its attention to the non-HR data. The team initiated a discovery process with the key holders of data—finance, marketing, customer service, business development, and operations—to find the metrics that are most relevant to the way Lowe's business operates.

Multiple meetings, facilitated by HR, were conducted during the course of a six-week period. In addition to gathering data, these meetings were important to establish credibility and buy-in. In the meetings, data holders had the opportunity to ask questions about how their information interacts with data from other parts of the company. Each meeting was designed to share purpose, establish "what's in it for me" for stakeholders, identify data availability, clarify outcomes, and, of course, address the skeptics. Even with leadership buy-in and HR as the facilitators, gathering all of the data from multiple sources required both patience and persuasion.

At the conclusion of the discovery process, the cross-functional team developed a people value linkage blueprint to document the data that were available, evaluate the quality of the data, and provide a road map for the model (see Exhibit 1.2). This blueprint also captured all of the expectations, or hypotheses, from the key stakeholders. These expectations translated into various stakeholders' perceptions. Some examples included the expectation that there would be a causal linkage between engagement and customer satisfaction and the expectation that the level of employee engagement would drive a reduction in accident and shrinkage rates. These expectations became the first set of hypotheses that the resulting models would measure.

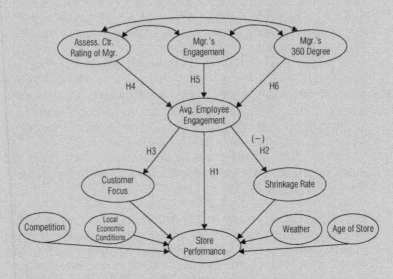

Exhibit 1.2 Lowe's First Store Model Blueprint
Source: Reprinted with permission from Lowe's

(Continued)

Step 3: Building behind the Firewall

Because most financial and operational data are too sensitive to take off site, the modeling itself took place within company firewalls with a two-part consultant analysis team consisting of a statistician and a business strategist. The combination of these two minds ensured that relationships tested in the model reflect both statistical accuracy and the reality of business.

The modeling process began with collecting all of these data from the various data holders in the several systems and cleaning it before merging it into one cohesive system. Lowe's included nearly 600 variables in the initial data set to be analyzed. The team used a combination of correlations, factor analysis, and regression to reduce the number of variables to the most predictive in each core area on the blueprint. For example, analysis determined which observed variables had the most predictive impact to be used to measure important metrics in retail, such as store performance and customer focus.

Structural equation modeling (a statistical technique that combines confirmatory factor analysis and path analysis) was then used to build and test the model created in the blueprint. Structural equation modeling is a deductive technique that tests a predetermined model. Most organizations have already chosen a structure and ways to interact within that structure to maximize business results. Decisions are made within organizations with express purposes. Deductive models allow organizations to test how well their structure and processes are working.

The process allows for revisions to the blueprint as variables are added or removed and for the testing of more than one model as new information is presented. The final model is constructed through creating different versions and testing each with different theoretical assumptions to look at new relationships that make sense in the context of the company. The model continues to be adapted until it reflects the best fit.

When the structural equation modeling process was complete, Lowe's had several core models that clearly delineated data correlations and causal linkages and the strength of those relationships (see Exhibit 1.3).

In this model, ovals indicate an item that is constructed of multiple variables, and rectangles indicate individual variables. Lines with arrows on both ends are co-varying relationships, meaning that the two items have an impact on each other. Lines with arrows pointing in one direction indicate that one item is affecting the other. The numeric values are regression error terms that show how much impact one item has on another (for example, if A affects B with a score of 0.14, then when A moves one unit, B will move 0.14). Positive values indicate that when one item goes up, the other item will

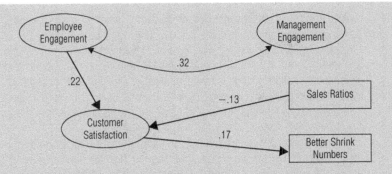

Exhibit 1.3 One of Lowe's First Core Models
Source: Reprinted with permission from Lowe's

also go up. Negative values indicate that when one item goes up, the other item will go down.

Once the base models were established, Lowe's was able to quantify the results into tangible financial impact measures within the organization and then further refine the models over time with additional metrics and insights. In this stage, the models are used to answer critical questions, such as

- Training increases cost, but it also should influence efficiency. How does that play out in reality, based on a company's actual financial results?
- Leadership tenure and staffing levels should contribute to customer satisfaction, but do they?
- What is the most effective HR program or investment to increase customer satisfaction?

Step 4: Identifying Performance Themes with Executive Buy-In

On development of the initial models, the researchers and Lowe's HR team conducted a working session with the data holders to fully explore the implications and refine the model. The team validated the model and the results and then analyzed the data to make sure it was pulling out the right initial themes that existed across the enterprise.

Lowe's was careful to focus on key strategic themes to ensure that management would focus on business priorities with the follow-up engagement action planning. Once the themes were understood from an HR perspective, they were shared with the executive team. Through dialogue with the executive team, enterprise-wide themes were agreed on and then shared with each function (finance, operations, and so on).

(Continued)

Although the executive team was supportive of value linkage's objectives, some questioned whether models could establish the cause-effect relationships. Because the models were built in concert with finance, operations, and research, the insights were acknowledged from functional stakeholders. This cross-functional design is essential to validity, as well as to acceptance. With this acceptance, Lowe's was able to use the models to prove a direct connection between engagement and customer satisfaction and the linkages to revenue, shrink rates, and a number of other areas.

Lowe's started the review and buy-in process with the HR leadership team, then with the executive staff, including the CEO, the functional leaders across the board, and then down to the workforce. The concept of working at the enterprise level helped to get agreement and work across silos.

The models were used to identify areas with the strongest relationships and greatest impact on Lowe's business priorities. These models became a foundation for prioritization of effort—influential in decision making for the HR team and operators within the organization. The models were then finalized, and the sharing and buy-in process across the organization began.

Step 5: Cascading Results and Taking Action

Many organizations find it difficult to disseminate value linkage data and results. The impact on performance is measured over time and is often part of a larger change initiative. A key success factor at Lowe's was sharing a combination of the visual models, simple charts and graphs and themes that represented the findings of the complex statistical models, and then communicating the findings in concrete financial measures that held meaning for key operators.

There are two ways to approach data sharing and follow-up. A functional approach allows individual business units to choose their own focus. An organizational approach looks at themes across the enterprise and provides direction to the functions. Lowe's chose an organizational approach to allow the time to educate the organization and business units on how to use the data and enhance control of the change process. In retail-focused operations—where operational excellence is a top priority—the tendency is to fix and deploy something as quickly as possible. Keeping the results at the thematic level within the enterprise ensured that the HR and operations components were created simultaneously to drive systemic and holistic change.

During the last five years, Lowe's has placed significant focus on employee engagement, and now it has permeated across the entire organization. Every business leader and each business unit believe in the importance of engagement and want to know how their workforce perceives them. Employees want to know how the decisions and investments the organization is making affect not only themselves but customers and the corporate infrastructure.

Now at Lowe's, management teams are eager to receive their information and, in the spirit of healthy competition, are energized to raise engagement. HR continues to partner with management teams to help maintain focus on key areas with the greatest impact on both engagement and the business.

Step 6: Evolving the Model

Lowe's conducted employee research to ask the workforce for input, by theme, to determine what employees needed to drive engagement in these priority areas. Lowe's used its employee communication platform to collect employee input, as well as to communicate their engagement investments. In some cases, employees wanted changes that Lowe's would not be able to provide, and it was important to be transparent and show that the engagement priorities were aligned to the business priorities.

After Lowe's collected employee input for priorities and action planning, it continued to build out its linkage models with more data. Within Lowe's, the focus has also grown beyond employee engagement to begin testing the impact of other HR programs that were determined to be essential to enhancing engagement. HR programs that support leadership development, enhance work-life balance, and foster diversity and inclusion can all be built and tested within the existing models to see their impact on engagement and ultimately on the bottom line. With each new data set, new hypotheses can be tested and new relationships proved.

In addition, during the first year of modeling, Lowe's conducted quarterly stratified sample surveys measuring employee engagement that mapped to financial quarters. This enabled the analytical team to create models that could account for lags and leads and to determine which drivers and relationships stayed constant over time or weakened, based on changes in the economy and the market. For example, did increased engagement in quarter 1 lead to improved customer satisfaction in quarter 1, or did it lag until quarter 2? How long did the effects of increased engagement last? This quarterly approach to modeling throughout the operational and financial year enabled the analytical team to test for seasonality and ebbs and flows of sales that are common to the retail setting.

This approach helps determine questions that need to be explored further or new questions that need to be asked. The models are designed to be

(Continued)

adapted and improved to reflect the constantly changing economy, work environment, market demands, and employee relationships.

Future Role for Value Linkage at Lowe's

Today, Lowe's has captured the impact of employee attitudes and how this affects the business—this is a milestone step for the HR business function. Lowe's is beginning to translate these models into forward-looking, predictive analytics.

Value linkage is a key step in the journey toward predictive analytics. Lowe's sees the next stage, which includes forecasting retention and productivity issues and the corresponding financial impact to make predictive investments for ongoing improvements. To reach this stage, Lowe's will need to continue to build out models with more details—market demographics, employee behavioral data, forecasts, and so on. Lowe's wants to know with a high degree of probability how the workforce will behave and the levers to pull for higher productivity—to predicatively analyze business from a human capital perspective.

SUMMARY

Human capital is the most important differentiator of a modern company. We are at a moment in time where theories about human capital, the amount of data available, and the computing power necessary to deal with the data are radically changing how business is done. We present the continuum of analytics, based on what we see in practice. All of analytics are useful: data ranges from anecdotes to hard operational data interpreted with statistics. Anecdotes add stories and context to your reports. Yet the rigorous analysis that provides true impact and helps you optimize your investments is the most important goal in the analysis of human capital. It is necessary to take your company into the next century.

NOTES

1. "Gartner Recession," *The Register* (October 18, 2011), retrieved April 2, 2012, from www.theregister.co.uk/2011/10/18/gartner_recession.

2. E. Brynjolfsson, L. M. Hitt, and H. H. Kim, *Strength in Numbers: How Does Data-Driven Decision Making Affect Firm Performance?* (April 22, 2011), retrieved June 1, 2012, from Social Science Research Network, http://papers.ssrn .com/sol3/papers.cfm?abstract_id=1819486&http://www.google.com/url? sa=t&rct=j&q=&esrc=s&source=web&cd=16&ved=0CFsQFjAFOAo&url= http%3A%2F%2Fpapers.ssrn.com%2Fsol3%2FDelivery.cfm%2FSSRN_ ID1968725_code1376648.pdf%3Fabstractid%3D1819486&ei=Q.

3. T. H. Davenport, J. G. Harris, and R. Morison, *Analytics at Work: Smarter Decisions, Better Results* (Boston, MA: Harvard Business Press, 2010).

4. R. O. Brinkerhoff, *The Success Case Method: Find Out Quickly What's Working and What's Not* (San Francisco: Berrett-Koehler Publishers, 2003).

5. R. S. Kaplan and D. P. Norton, *The Balanced Scorecard: Translating Strategy into Action* (Boston, MA: Harvard Press, 1996).

6. R. Griffeth and P. W. Hom, *Retaining Valued Employees* (Thousand Oaks, CA: Sage, 2001).

7. W. F. Cascio and J. W. Boudreau, *Investing in People: Financial Impact of Human Resource Initiatives* (Upper Saddle River, NJ: Pearson, 2008).

8. R. S. Kaplan and D. P. Norton, *Strategy Maps—Converting Intangible Assets into Tangible Outcomes* (Boston, MA: Harvard Business School Press, 2004).

9. Towers Perrin, "Employee Engagement Underpins Business Transformation" (September 2009), retrieved June 21, 2012, from www.towersperrin .com/tp/getwebcachedoc?country=gbr&webc=GBR/2008/200807/TP_ISR_ July08.pdf.

10. A. Fink, "New Trends in Human Capital Research and Analytics," *People & Strategy* 33, no. 2 (2010): 14–21.

CHAPTER **2**

Alignment

"A senior manager hoping to influence behavior has no stronger lever than his or her choice of measures."

—Scott Anthony, Mark Johnson, Joseph Sinfield, and
Elizabeth Altman, *An Innovator's Guide to Growth*[1]

A lignment is a popular topic of conversation in human resources today. Yet few HR leaders are able to follow through on true alignment with their business. So what is alignment? Alignment is a plan that explicitly connects investments to strategic goals via the metrics. Alignment is about finding the relevant stakeholders in the company and connecting them to the parts in that plan. Alignment positions human resources as a strategic partner in support of the business. To follow through on alignment means that HR understands and helps drive business goals (rather than the converse, where business drives HR goals). It requires a fundamental shift in thinking—from HR as a cost center to HR as an investment, a business partner, and an important seat at the C-suite table.

It is crucial for HR to design people investments that drive business goals. We do not think HR can design those investments without systematically evaluating and improving on the impact of those investments on key metrics. For human capital investments to be truly successful, they must be aligned with business goals and, ultimately, to the organization's strategy. Organizations spend billions annually on

31

human capital investments. All too often, HR interventions are designed without business outcomes in mind. Although they may be worthwhile investments, in and of themselves, the money is wasted if the investment does not make a strategic connection back to the business.

The value of alignment is multifaceted. To be considered a strategic partner is certainly good for HR's reputation, but more important, it ensures that HR is driving business performance. If you investigate leading companies, you will learn that the vast majority of them have aligned their HR functions with business strategy. Laurie Bassi has defined the "good company" as an organization that is a good employer and a good steward for the interests of its community. Bassi puts this concept to the test by managing an investment fund, Bassi Investments, that has invested in these good companies. Its fund has outperformed the S&P 500 during the last 10 years. Her conclusion is that companies that invest in their people outperform their peers.[2]

Finally, alignment enables you to measure and improve the investment's impact. The alignment process outlined in this chapter involves defining success for an investment, gaining stakeholder buy-in to the indicators of success, and ensuring that success is measurable. Doing so reduces the risk of the investment by designing for the outcomes you want to drive and assuring the support of your business partners whom will be impacted.

Not every human capital investment is going to drive bottom-line profitability. For example, many investments are purely to satisfy compliance issues. There are also cultural investments that contribute to maintaining corporate values and a certain type of workplace. These are seen as worthwhile if the business leaders have placed an emphasis on these types of cultural issues. Also, a strategic connection back to the business does not have to mean profits. Succession planning and leadership development initiatives are vital to the future of any organization, but they are more difficult (although not impossible) to link to a financial metric. We still consider this a type of alignment, even though the investments to which the key performance indicators link are intangible.

THE STAKEHOLDER WORKSHOP: CREATING THE RIGHT CLIMATE FOR ALIGNMENT

At the beginning of a measurement project, we gather key stakeholders together for a formal stakeholder meeting to ensure that people investments are aligned with business outcomes and strategic goals. Typically a half-day in duration, these meetings use a guided discussion format to define measurable success for the investment and collaboratively design the measurement plan (details of which will be addressed in Chapter 3). Gaining the key stakeholder insights is critical for making sure your HR investments are aligned with organizational goals, but it also has a secondary purpose that is equally important. A goal of the discussion is to gain the key stakeholders' buy-in to the investment itself and the logic underlying the plan for measurement. Doing so ensures that stakeholders are part of the process, rather than potential critics later on. The guided discussion follows the Measurement Map process (also described in Chapter 3) as a way to visually describe the chain of evidence from investment to business impact to strategic goals. An important point here is that the discussion does not begin with the question, "What metrics do we need to track?" Rather it is about defining measurable success first and creating causal links between the investment and the strategic goal(s). Once that is done, it is relatively straightforward to identify the metrics and data sources needed for measurement.

ALIGNING STAKEHOLDERS

Stakeholder alignment is HR's tool for aligning with the business. Aligning the stakeholders allows you to benefit from the expertise of the people affected by the human capital investment, while gaining their buy-in to the investment and its measurement plan. Stakeholder alignment ensures that the logic behind your study design will resonate with business outcomes. Stakeholder alignment offers a forum for hearing the stakeholders' individual issues and concerns. Stakeholder meetings can also tell you if the links between leading indicators and business results are accurate. The important issue is that stakeholders need to discuss the behavior they need from their employees, the observable (that is, measurable) parts of a business process, and how the parts can inform actual strategic decisions and behaviors. You will also need their help to get the necessary data. You may be surprised by how much you learn from their collaboration—for many companies, a measurement stakeholder meeting is the first time these particular individuals have been in the room together (or on a Web conference, if they are in dispersed locations). By initiating this type of cross-functional gathering, HR can play a role in breaking down organizational silos and encouraging collaboration among business units. Stakeholder alignment is best sought at the outset of planning for an investment. Even if you did not get stakeholder alignment before deploying the investment, stakeholders' participation in developing a measurement plan is still essential to successfully evaluating business impact.

Stakes are high simply because people in complex organizations have different points of view and biases. Bringing them together may surface the hidden conflicts, so you must be able to navigate a variety of opinions and skepticism. Sometimes people disagree over how to define success, hesitate to commit to specifics, or disagree over what metrics should be involved. This can reflect a hesitancy to have one's own work reviewed. Others show a well-meaning but misplaced respect for individuals and their privacy. Statistics are about how groups of people are likely to perform, not a judgment on individuals. When group impacts are measured through optimization, an investment is usually of value to at least some of the groups being measured. Groups that do not benefit may be relieved of having to participate in training that doesn't help them or may receive some new investment tailored to help them succeed.

As you lead a stakeholder meeting, our preferred method is to lead an "appreciative inquiry" into the interests and contributions of the group. Appreciative inquiry (AI) is an organization development method that emphasizes what an organization does well, rather than eliminating what it does badly.[3] AI asks questions such as, "What is working well?" and "What is good about the current set up?" AI focuses on three key activities: discovering, dreaming, and designing. Bringing out those aspects and addressing sources of conflict and skepticism will create buy-in and enthusiasm for the investment and its attendant measurement plan.

WHO ARE YOUR STAKEHOLDERS?

There are several components to planning a successful stakeholder meeting, beginning with the attendee list. An incomplete gathering of stakeholders may result in a measurement plan that is incomplete, which weakens the evidence of business impact. The attendee list for a stakeholder meeting will understandably vary, based on the structure of the organization and the investment itself. In general, the stakeholders are those interested in the outcomes and improvement of the investment, as well as those who can help identify and gain access to the data necessary for a measurement initiative. They will be drawn from both the solution providers (e.g., the HR practitioners who are responsible for the investment) and those who benefit (e.g., the operations managers whose departments participate in the investment).

There are several main reasons to include individuals from outside the HR group:

- Alignment is about getting the company to work together as a team. The process requires information and buy-in from different areas about what the strategic goals are, what the outcomes are, and how they can be measured.

- People outside HR may have expertise (and strong feelings) about the objectives of the human capital investment. Both their expertise and their feelings are important. Representation of the group or business unit whose investment is included is of particular importance.

- Data can come from multiple places in the organization, and different stakeholders can provide access to it.

- There are people outside of HR who make decisions, such as whether to cut, maintain, or expand funding. They are likely to be interested in the results of the measurement project. Some people like to be surprised with results from a study. Most people do not like to be surprised with results from a study, so including them at an early stage is important.

- Cost and valuation issues may be crucial for gaining acceptance of the results of the impact study by anyone outside of HR. If so, your estimates and assumptions should be vetted with the parties who have expertise and a stake in the process. Remember, although your analysis techniques may be beyond the understanding of the audience for your eventual report, value estimates almost never are. A dispute over a value estimate can derail an otherwise excellent report on the impact of an investment.

Consider which stakeholders are appropriate for the particular investment. If you are designing a new immersive sales training simulation, you will want to consult a few of your colleagues in the sales department. After all, they are the ones sending their direct reports to the training and are hoping to realize a benefit from it. For a leadership development investment, consider who will feel the effects of the program—division managers, perhaps? Beyond these specialty participants, involve representatives from finance, business operations, field operations, and IT (as they are typically closest with the data you will need) as applicable. Consider everyone who will be directly touched by the investment and those whose cooperation you will need to obtain data.

In general, participants for the stakeholder meeting will come from

- HR department (including training personnel, if applicable)
- Subject matter experts
- Finance
- Operations/IT
- Management

Most measurement projects will offer opportunities to express results financially. When you design a measurement plan, strongly consider your source for financial information and involve a knowledgeable stakeholder early in the process. For example, if the investment is a sales training program, you should involve the VP or the director of sales—someone who understands the metrics the sales department uses to measure the performance of its people. Bringing these individuals on board early in the planning stages—either for the investment itself or for the measurement project—enhances credibility and cooperation within an organization. Disagreement about financial assumptions can challenge the credibility of the results of any measurement project, thereby calling into question the credibility of the investment itself.

When building a stakeholder meeting invitation list, it is important to ask high-level stakeholders about the source of their data. It is often the case that a trusted subordinate has been providing business intelligence to an executive for some time; if that is the case, that individual should be included. These subordinates may have the word *analyst* or *database* somewhere in their titles and know what data are available in the organization, as well as how and from whom to get data. Once you have attained the political buy-in to gain access to data, the person with his or her hands on the data is the most direct route to receiving what you need. When the data analyst working with you connects to this person, that's when a project really shifts into high gear.

WHAT SHOULD YOU ACCOMPLISH IN A STAKEHOLDER MEETING?

Participants will often say that the stakeholder meeting is one of the most productive working sessions they have attended. We prefer the word *workshop*, because it has a collaborative, exciting feel. It would seem obvious to get people together from disparate parts of the organization to occasionally compare notes, but, as you likely know, other priorities often interfere with doing so. After all, getting eight people together for a four-hour meeting is almost a week's worth of productivity. The conversations on business processes that occur during a stakeholder meeting can reveal new relationships and viewpoints with benefits well beyond the investment and measurement project. Human resources and learning functional units hear their goals being stated in clear, unambiguous language that speaks to the concerns of the business as a whole and moves beyond the day-to-day details of managing a department. The units of measurement are one of the best ways to talk about what concrete aspects of behavior are desired.

Aligning an investment in people with business outcomes and communicating about those goals in a common language is the chief accomplishment of a productive stakeholder meeting. These goals are what we refer to as the definition of success for the investment. A stakeholder meeting should leave everyone with a clear idea of what needs to be measured, the value of that information, and what could be done with it. When the meeting is complete, there should be a clear understanding of the following points:

- The intended outcomes of the investment.
- Who the participants in the study are (i.e., the audience for the investment).
- The relevant metrics and sources of data.
- What demographic variables (e.g., tenure, location, education) are useful, in the sense that they
  - Affect the values of the metrics.
  - Are fair game for decision making.
  - Mediate or affect the value of any interventions being studied.
- A list of existing data within the organization relevant to the project, as well as any data that need to be collected for the study.
- Hypotheses about the measurement project that make concrete predictions and can be verified or falsified.

A whiteboard or a flipchart is invaluable for capturing progress and creating the measurement map of your goals. At the end of the session, a camera phone can be used to capture the material written on boards. Keep in mind that any information generated can be useful in some way, even if there are important questions that cannot be answered. Many organizations simply accept missing data, instead of formulating a plan to collect and share that data. However, you may be in a position to propose new data collection mechanisms. Situations with important missing data represent opportunities for improvement.

A simple question can open the conversation: "What would you like to see people do differently as a result of this investment?" The answers will start broad; for example, for sales training, "we want to see our reps sell more products." For a leadership development initiative, "we want to see our managers become more effective leaders." For a performance management program, "we want people within disparate divisions to feel like they're part of a unified whole." Don't worry if, at this early stage in the meeting, these goals are vague and unquantifiable. At this point, you want to get your stakeholders' ideas flowing and ensure that everyone has a common understanding of what the investment is trying to accomplish. Once you have gained agreement on these high-level goals, you can take steps to make sure they are measurable.

Once the big ideas are on the table, probe deeper. If managers complete the leadership development initiative and become more effective leaders, how will we know it? What types of things might they do differently than they are doing now? What business problems related to the targeted audience's performance would you expect this intervention to solve? A good motivator is to ask whether the stakeholders believe that investments cause desired change simply as a matter of pure faith or whether there are things they see in the world around them. Pure faith, for business initiatives, is never the answer. Once observable behavior or facts become the focus, the necessary attitude is in place to follow those changes.[4] A simple question to ask is, "How would you know if that happened?" These objectives can be organized into *measurable* and *nonmeasurable* outcomes.

Measurable outcomes are those that have some specific quantity that can be counted. You may describe your goal as improving sales without describing the exact variable to be considered. Study other benefits as well, such as retention or increased engagement. Although these may not be built into the fabric of the program, they are typically effects of a successful investment.

Our process focuses on tangible, quantifiable outcomes, but there are plenty of good reasons to invest in people that are not so measurable. If there are nonmeasurable outcomes, explicitly list them. Just because they are not measurable does not mean they cannot be articulated. Some nonmeasurable outcomes would include

- Transforming company culture
- Improving communication skills
- Enhancing leadership skills
- Gender and diversity awareness

Sometimes when articulating the nonmeasurable outcomes, metrics may become apparent. This allows you to move them to measurable outcomes. The best approach is to assume that an outcome is measurable and give it considerable thought before determining otherwise.

Once the goals are clear, it is important to gain agreement on an estimate of how much of a difference in impact or behavior is expected. What performance improvements can be realistically expected from various investments? Could a job aid reduce errors in a call center by 5 percent? Is a sales increase of one unit per person, per month possible because of the investment? Committing to specific numbers may make your stakeholders uncomfortable, but it is an important discussion to have. First, it makes the stakeholders articulate and visualize what they hope to achieve with the investment, so it will create subtle changes in how they feel about the investment itself. Second, if the project does not produce significant results in a particular area, there are methods for examining the data to determine what results *could* have been detected. For example, when you know a little about the data and some statistics, you could say that a 5 percent improvement could have been detected or a 15 percent improvement could have been detected, but not smaller ones. That allows you to have a broader, more interesting dialogue about sample sizes, as well as whether the training might be producing positive results, but ones that are too small to appear in your analysis.

It is best to phrase these changes as hypotheses so that specific questions can be answered in a concrete way, rather than simply talking about investigating areas and seeing what arises. Your hypotheses should be able to be proved or disproved with data. Writing hypotheses makes everything more concrete: What data need to be collected? What questions need to be answered? What actions are foreseeable after analyzing the data and answering the questions? Rather than saying, "I want to know if sales training works," think about some focused questions:

- Does the sales training produce an increase in units sold?
- Does the sales training produce an increase in per-unit profitability?

- Is sales training more useful for associates in large stores or small stores?
- Can salespeople relate positive anecdotes about using something they learned?

From these business questions, you may develop as a hypothesis: "Sales training will produce an increase in units sold and per-unit profitability." Once all hypotheses are defined, you are ready to start discussing what, specifically, to measure.

DECIDING WHAT TO MEASURE WITH YOUR STAKEHOLDERS

There are a number of curious facts affecting measurements. First, the fact that people know they are being measured tends to make them behave differently. This was first noted during a study at AT&T's Western Electric plant in Cicero, Illinois, and is referred to as the Hawthorne effect.[5] Workers who were subjected to better lighting conditions improved in productivity. The first assumption was that better lights were responsible—until a control group that received poorer lighting also improved. Further manipulations confirmed that the workers simply responded to the attention that they were receiving.

When measurement is mixed with incentives, the measurement itself may become questionable. If you incentivize for the wrong thing, the results can be disastrous. The Department of Defense once measured programmer productivity by the number of lines of code written. On some level, this may be useful, although software engineers have long known that for any given problem, concise, elegant code beats redundant, sloppy code any day of the week (although sloppy code has far more lines). One company rewarded programmers for the number of bugs fixed in the common code library. This led to programmers checking their code into the common library early so that bugs they would have fixed previously on their desktop could be credited in their metrics.[6]

Measurement can happen at many levels and in many ways. Consider customer satisfaction: you can count retained customers, count the number of new referrals, send out a survey to customers, interview random samples of customers, count hits on the support section of the website, or count the costs on returned products. Metrics that have a concrete count and a dollar value are *business* metrics, and those that predict or indicate the underlying phenomena, such as potential sales in a pipeline, are *leading indicators.*

An important point to remember here is not to limit yourself to the data you think are easily accessible. Consider the broader scope of what you would like to learn (i.e., your hypotheses) and what data sources are needed in order to do so. The data may come from across the business—not just within the HR department. Gaining an understanding of what information is available and what is required to gain access to it is another key goal of the stakeholder meeting. Ideally, you should pull together the owners of the necessary data or at least the people who can make political connections for you to gain access to it. We explore this in much greater detail in Chapter 4.

When an investment has a direct line of sight to business goals, it is rather easy to ensure business alignment. For example, sales training is generally deployed to increase revenue, new accounts, and/or gross margin. Customer call center training is intended to decrease average call-handling time or escalation of calls to a supervisor or to up-sell a product or a service. In each of these cases, the value of the desired business result is rather easy to calculate. Yet how do you align investments that have an indirect line of sight (i.e., the softer HR investments)? Leadership development programs generally take a long time to deploy and have less obvious business outcomes. The same could be said for mentoring programs, performance management systems, and tuition assistance programs. Aligning these types of investments with business results is not always easy to do, but it is eminently possible with help from leading indicators.

LEADING INDICATORS

In cases where there is an indirect line of sight to the business metrics, we align the investment by finding leading indicators. Leading indicators are typically nonfinancial values that tell you if you are on the right track. If I am a real estate agent, my business metric is how many house sales I close and the affiliated sales commission (my income). Leading indicators that would let me know I'm on the way to having a successful year are my number of active listings and open houses. The more listings and open houses I have, the better my chances of closing sales.

In many cases, leading indicators can point to early course corrections to ensure that you reach the desired business outcomes. Some examples of HR leading indicators are

- Employee engagement scores
- Internal/external fill rates
- Hires from targeted schools
- Performance review scores
- Implemented improvement ideas
- Number of complaints

Suppose an increase in employee engagement scores is a leading indicator in the causal chain to business impact for a three-year leadership development initiative. At the end of year one, employee engagement scores for the participants in the leadership development program decline. This is an example of a leading indicator highlighting a need for course corrections, which is, of course, the great advantage of leading indicators—they provide data while the situation is easier to improve. You would want to look into why the engagement scores went down (perhaps through a survey or interviews with participants) and see if there is some element of the leadership development program that needs to be adjusted. Or, perhaps you determine that the decline in engagement scores was the result of some outside factor—company-wide restructuring, perhaps, or a downtown in the economy. In this situation, you may want to see whether participants had less of a decline than nonparticipants. Or you may determine that employee engagement is no longer a valid leading indicator of success and may collaborate with your stakeholders to decide whether to remove it. For example, satisfaction surveys are not generally regarded as a useful tool in military basic training.

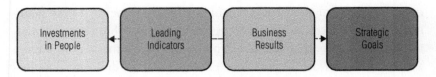

Exhibit 2.1 Alignment from People Investments to Strategic Goals

BUSINESS IMPACT

Leading indicators should point toward business impact metrics. Business impact metrics, commonly referred to as key performance indicators (KPIs), are tied to a financial value. If a metric does not have a financial value, it is not a business impact metric. Some common examples of business impact metrics are

- Turnover
- Customer loyalty
- Revenue per full-time employee
- Workers' compensation costs
- Productivity
- Cost avoidance

Exhibit 2.1 shows the alignment from people investments to strategic goals.

ASSIGNING FINANCIAL VALUES TO "INTANGIBLES"

Studies based on financial terms have a wider audience appeal and a clearer value proposition than those that merely show a unit-by-unit impact. Some values, such as sales revenue, map directly to a dollar value, because they are already in dollars. In other cases, you need to be persistent in your approach to finding values. For some intangible benefits, it is difficult to assign a concrete value, but the process of linking leading indicators to business impact metrics often allows an intangible benefit to be assigned a financial value, preferably one conservative enough to satisfy all stakeholders.

Sometimes the translation into dollar terms requires some creative assumptions, rather than just number crunching. For example, one mentoring program spanned an entire organization, including people in completely different jobs. We chose merit-based performance bonuses for a metric. Our argument was that for someone to receive an extra dollar in pay, he or she must have created at least a dollar's worth of value for the company.

Collaborating with associates in finance or accounting can be very useful at this stage. At a minimum, it assists you in learning to speak their language. Collaboration with finance facilitates your ability to take that extra step to translate the measure into dollars. Consider a 5-point customer satisfaction rating. How much does a customer who gave you a 5 spend in a year, compared to the customers who gave you a 4? Compute averages for each rating category, and then look at the differences between them. You can now talk about the value of a program to increase customer satisfaction. With regard to employee engagement scores, suppose you know the score is linked to turnover. For every magnitude increase in employee engagement, turnover decreases by a certain percentage. Most organizations have a per-head cost of turnover they can apply to gain a financial metric. Therefore, reducing turnover is linked more broadly to the organization's strategic goal of cutting costs.

DEFINING YOUR PARTICIPANTS

Once you have identified your goals, leading indicators, and business metrics, you need to decide on the participants in your study. We use the term *participants* to describe everyone whose data you will measure—not just those who participated in the investment. As long as the "control group" is comparable to the test group, you might as well get as many participants as you can. They are either the targets of the human capital investment or similar individuals who are not going to receive the investment in the study time frame. Chapter 6 includes a more detailed discussion of how to establish control and test groups for your study.

To data analysts, a participant is just a unit that generates data at regular intervals. In most cases, participants are people employed by the company, but occasionally other entities may be involved if applicable data are available. For example, sales channel partners may be participants in a sales training study. Doctors writing prescriptions may be participants in a pharmaceutical training study. Occasionally, these participants do not map neatly to data sources. For example, we have seen programs where managers were trained, but the managers' performance was not able to be tied to individual data; the branch office produces data. In this case, the study did not measure the impact of giving training to managers, per se, but instead, the impact of giving a branch office a trained manager. In the simple case where each branch office has exactly one trained manager, the mapping is pretty simple, and redefining the participant may sound silly. However, if there are multiple managers, some trained and some not, the mapping may be a little more complicated. It is good planning to decide from the beginning how you will handle the situation.

You should be able to define who a participant is and count how many received or did not receive the intervention. As your understanding of the project progresses, your distinctions about who is or isn't a participant will become more sophisticated. For example, are nonunion or temporary employees included? What about those who have been there less than three years? These decisions should be documented as you proceed.

Larger numbers tend to generate results that are more statistically sound. However, do not let a small population deter you from measuring. By doing this alignment work, you can still gain great insight into impact, whether your population is in the thousands, hundreds, or dozens. Chapter 6 will discuss this topic in more detail.

RIO TINTO'S CONTRACTOR MANAGEMENT SYSTEM USING ANALYSIS TO SOLVE A LARGE BUSINESS ISSUE

But as always, let me start with safety. Our safety performance was marred by six fatalities at our managed operations last year and one earlier this year. These were all terrible tragedies that are deeply felt by the families, friends, and colleagues of those who died. It means we must redouble our efforts to make ours a zero harm company. I believe this to be an achievable goal and having everyone go home

safe at the end of every day is at the heart of my vision for our company. The road to zero harm is challenging, especially during times of major expansion, but I will not be satisfied until all of our locations are entirely injury-free.
—Address by Tom Albanese, chief executive, Rio Tinto, Brisbane, May 10, 2012, Rio Tinto Limited Annual General Meeting

Rio Tinto is a leading international mining group. Its approach to mining is to focus on the development of first-class ore bodies into large, long-life, and efficient operations, capable of sustaining competitive advantage through business cycles. Rio Tinto's interests are diverse, both in geography and in product. The group works in some of the world's most difficult terrains and climates. Most of its assets are in Australia and North America, but Rio Tinto also operates in Europe, South America, Asia, and Africa. Its businesses include open pit and underground mines, mills, refineries, and smelters, as well as a number of research and service facilities. Wherever Rio Tinto operates, health and safety are always the first priority. All of Rio Tinto's group businesses put sustainable development at the heart of their operations.

Its goal is zero harm for all of the people who work in their group. Regrettably, they have not reached that goal. Since 2002, it has had 49 fatalities (see Exhibit 2.2), with a large number of them contractors. Indeed, 66 percent of the fatalities in 2008 were contractors. At that point, Rio Tinto began to focus more on its contractor safety information to see if there was evidence that these workers were not operating as safely as its "regular" workforce and if so, why. Rio Tinto found that when it plotted out its All Injury Frequency Rate (AIFR), there was just such a trend. The rate of injury had decreased from 2002 to 2009; however, there was a consistent gap between the two workforces, with contractors consistently having more injuries than "regular" employees (see Exhibit 2.3).

Rio Tinto also recognized the scale of the issue. By going into its Health, Safety, and Environment (HSE) database, the company was able to track exposure hours in order to get an estimate of the number of contractors being used across product groups and corporate functions. Rio Tinto discovered that it had hired the equivalent of approximately 50,000 contractors from nearly 9,000 vendors in 40 different countries. Rio Tinto then delved into its procurement systems. By analyzing service contracts for the last 12 months, Rio Tinto was able to report that it had spent in excess of $3 billion on contractor services. This was clearly one of the largest spend categories for Rio Tinto and one that it knew little about on a group-wide basis.

(Continued)

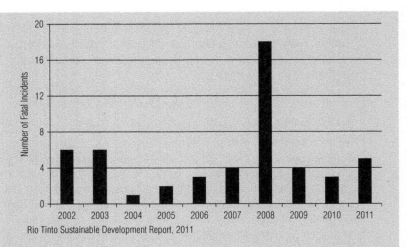

Rio Tinto Sustainable Development Report, 2011

Exhibit 2.2 Fatal Incidents
Reprinted with permission from Rio Tinto

Exhibit 2.3 All Injury Frequency Rate
Reprinted with permission from Rio Tinto

Rio Tinto's next step was to figure out how big an issue contractor management would be as it grew. To answer this question, Rio Tinto modeled the need for contract labor to meet its corporate objectives for growth. Taking into account the current workforce's production, growth objectives during the next 10 years, and expected attrition rates, Rio Tinto projected that it would need to increase the contractor workforce by more than 50,000. Contractors make up a critical and growing part of Rio Tinto's workforce. To be successful, the group needs to manage this workforce effectively. However, Rio Tinto realized that it did not have the "right" process and systems in place accomplish that task.

The challenge was irrefutable. Now the task became the identification of the causes and the development of a mitigation process that would eliminate the gap and lower the AIFR for contractors, while continuing to lower the rate of injury in Rio Tinto's entire workforce.

In addition to the safety issue described earlier, there were a number of commercial issues that were well-placed to be addressed through the approach Rio Tinto took to contractor management. The following list of issues includes those that were routinely observed across Rio Tinto sites:

Contractor Sourcing and Buying

- Size and scale not being fully leveraged, leading to higher than necessary contractor costs.
- Lack of contractor demand planning, leading to a limited ability to manage demand and source strategically.
- Lack of visibility of contractors needed, leading to logistics being a bottleneck to getting the "right" contractors on site at the right time (i.e., availability of travel and accommodation).

Contractor Management and Administration

- There were no comprehensive or consistently applied processes at a group level for using contractors and managing their day-to-day activities. This required each site to develop its own process with associated costs.
- The allocation of roles, responsibilities, and accountabilities for contractor management was unclear between business units and HSE, Procurement, and Human Resources functions.
- Where processes existed, not enough training had been provided to ensure that those involved in the management of contractors were aware of and adhered to these processes.

Once Rio Tinto had identified the broader issues, it was able to gain additional insight into areas it needed to address by going back to studies that had been conducted in prior years. Human Resources had conducted a contractor spend analysis, which gave visibility to the scale of the issue. The HSE team had a study that focused on the continuous management improvement of contractors. Ernst & Young had completed a three-year audit across 30 sites, focused on the various processes used to manage contractors. A benchmarking study that focused on contractor management had been completed by Accenture, the global management consulting firm, in 2009. All of these studies provided evidence to reinforce findings that

(Continued)

Rio Tinto faced a range of pressing challenges and critical risks relating to contractor management that needed to be addressed.

Rio Tinto took this large body of information from these multiple sources and consolidated it into four key challenge areas, as shown in Exhibit 2.4.

Challenges	Indicators
1. Lower HSE performance of contractors when compared with our employees (specifically for category 3 contractors)	• Average 30% gap in AIFR performance and 20% for Lost Time Injury Frequency Rate (LTIFR)
2. Lack of commercial rigor associated with the spend on contractors, resulting in increased costs and operational impacts through suboptimal performance	• Direct savings potential of 6–11% on contractor spend • Numerous sites operating with poor processes and limited compliance
3. Various risks arising from the lack of integrity in the processes used to engage and manage contractors	• Significant number of audited sites receiving marginal rating[1]
4. Limited ability to deal with any growth in the contractor segment of our workforce, or any potential structural changes weighted toward non-employee labor	• No reliable data on number of contractors, performance trends, or market dynamics • Significant parts of the contractor management processes performed across the business units are manual and resource intensive

Exhibit 2.4   Key Challenges and Evidence to Support
Reprinted with permission from Rio Tinto

Selecting a Pilot Site

Energy Resources of Australia (ERA) mines ore and produces uranium oxide at its Ranger open pit mine in Australia's Northern Territory. ERA's operations are subject to stringent environmental requirements and governmental oversight.

Due to its remoteness, it is extremely important for the ERA mine to plan for its workforce needs, which includes a significant portion of contractor labor. ERA understood that because of its size and the type of work that needed to be done, the majority of workers came from relatively small contract companies that did not have the safety training and focus that Rio Tinto expected. In addition, ERA understood that the proposed contractor management solution would address a number of safety audit findings.

Through the process of exploring a vendor management solution (VMS), Rio Tinto discovered that the introduction of this type of system could potentially save 5 percent to 10 percent of the total contractor cost.

When this information was presented to ERA's senior leadership, they recognized the potential for improved safety and commercial advantage that this approach offered and supported its development.

Where Rio Tinto Was in 2009

Rio Tinto's business units, numbering around 40 in total, employed a number of different approaches for managing contractors. These approaches were tactical in nature and, with one notable exception, did not attempt to address the issue of contractor management from "end-to-end." No single approach was sponsored at the group level for adoption across the organization. One business unit did provide an insight into a possible solution. It had dedicated resources managing contractors and had instituted changes that delivered excellent results. This included both the safety performance of its contractors and several other aspects of the commercial engagement process.

Rio Tinto deconstructed that approach and identified some best practices that could be introduced into its other business units. Rio Tinto was able to validate this approach with Hugo Bague (group executive, People & Organization) and Scott Singer (the head of Global Business Services), both of whom had prior experience with end-to-end contractor management in other companies. They were able to provide senior leadership sponsorship in a number of different areas. Without their leadership, getting this project "across the line" would have been impossible.

Three key elements of the approach worked in sync to deliver a sustainable shift in performance (see Exhibit 2.5).

When these business processes and tools are implemented together, they result in an organization that is well-resourced and has a dedicated focus on the day-to-day management of contractors. This includes the overall management of the expense, the third-party resources focusing on the administration activity, and the supervisory staff focused on work and HSE performance.

The approach required that an additional cost be incurred by the business units in the management of contractors associated with the VMS and managed service partner (MSP) program. However, these costs are more than offset by the significant savings that flowed through the improved controls and process discipline. Managing this cost is especially important for companies such as Rio Tinto, where the services spend is one of the largest areas of spend for the organization and where in the past its investment in actively managing this cost had been negligible. Individual

(Continued)

service engagements were typically small in nature (requiring approval at low levels), poorly defined, and executed with limited focus on the process disciplines that should be applied. The introduction of this system has provided senior management with an easy means of oversight and control.

Change	Impact
1. Establish dedicated roles to execute all administrative activity associated with the end-to-end contractor management processes: a. This can be accomplished through creation of internal specialist roles or	• Significant increase in process compliance and efficiency • Reduced burden on supervisory staff, allowing them to focus on work and health, safety, and environment (HSE) performance
b. Through the engagement of a dedicated third party service provider that is a managed service provider (MSP).	• Improved sustainability and process performance • Consistency in performance of the activities • Reduced risk of diluting focus due to competing priorities • Continuous improvement through link to industry best practice
2. Implement a specialized Web-based solution that is shared by Rio Tinto staff, vendors, and individual contractors and that fully enables the end-to-end contractor management processes. These solutions are known as a vendor management system (VMS).	• Shared solution fully enables the processes and allows them to be heavily streamlined • Extensive reporting capability empowers leaders to assess compliance and deliver savings • Vendor and contractor activity enables performance to be visible across sites and business units
3. Deploy streamlined and integrated leading practice processes that address the HSE and commerical issues.	• Increased efficiencies and controls throughout the process • Built-in, system-enabled checks and balances to address HSE requirements and commercial issues

Exhibit 2.5   Three Key Elements to Deliver a Sustainable Shift in Performance
Reprinted with permission from Rio Tinto

Developing a Group-Wide Approach

Rio Tinto's approach was designed to address the need for an end-to-end process for contractor management that is comprehensive in creating a well-documented set of business processes, policies, and guidelines. It also establishes a VMS solution that has been fully integrated with the Rio Tinto business solution (SAP).

Selecting a Vendor Management Solution and Managed Service Partner

A short list of "best in class" companies offering VMSs was organized and contacted. Two vendors were selected for an exhaustive, three-day-each, face-to-face review, where they were asked to present how their system would manage a number of different contractor management scenarios, present a detailed picture of their costing model, and respond to questions from a panel of internal experts representing the disciplines of Procurement, HSE, Human Resources, and Information Technology. Representatives of the pilot site, ERA, were also present to help ascertain the vendors' cultural fit. At the end of these reviews, the members of the selection team rated each vendor, and a partner for this work was selected.

A similar process was undertaken to identify "best in class" MSP vendors. Based on their response to the request for information, they were invited to respond to a request for proposals, and Rio Tinto selected an MSP to partner with it on the pilot.

As Rio Tinto expands this effort, it has taken the position that sites can staff the contract management process either internally or with an MSP. Rio Tinto has also not mandated a particular MSP, leaving this decision at the business unit level.

The end-to-end contractor management system (CMS) with benefits is shown in Exhibit 2.6.

Implementation

Rio Tinto identified the need for a change to the way it managed its contract employees, both from a safety and a commercial perspective, and using existing research, audit findings, and internal best practices to map out an approach. Then, going through a rigorous vendor selection process to ensure that it had the "right" partners to put this solution in place, Rio Tinto began the detailed and systematic process of ensuring that it implemented the solution successfully.

The implementation of the CMS occurred in four distinct stages.

Stage 1 (initiating) consisted of securing support for the work with the business unit management team. This was done by presenting the high-level analysis detailed earlier to corporate leadership. This gained the team the sponsorship of top management and paved the way for team members to gain access to business unit senior leadership. A series of meetings was held with them to share the evidence, the approach, the communication plan, and the commitment of the group to "fix" the issues they had with contractor management.

(Continued)

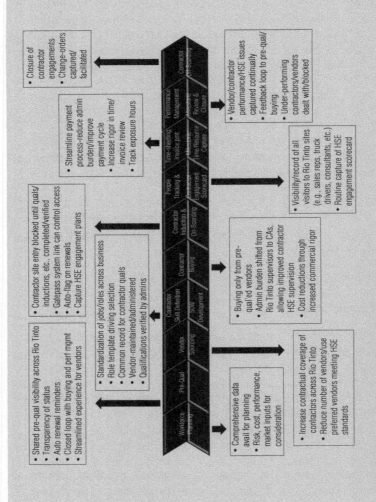

Exhibit 2.6 Key Features and Benefits Enabled
Reprinted with permission from Rio Tinto

Once they had this support, they performed the following stage 1 (initiating) tasks:

- Identified and named a business unit project manager.
- Identified all key stakeholders.
- Put a business unit steering committee in place.
- Secured VMS and MSP contracts/statement of work.
- Built a general communication plan.

Stage 2 (planning) focused on producing a vision of the future state of CMS within the business unit and a detailed plan to get there. This work was driven by a series of workshops that began the change management process through the collective building of the "To Be State." Businesses first shared what the best practices are for managing the end-to-end contractor management process and then worked with stakeholders to define the current state in terms of process, systems, and people. Once this had been accomplished, Rio Tinto was able to conduct a gap analysis, in terms of what needed to change in the process, the systems, and the people to achieve a best practice future state.

In addition to the To Be State workshop, Rio Tinto also brought its stakeholders together to identify all of the major risks and obstacles to the success of the project that needed to be taken into consideration in the rest of the planning. Rio Tinto developed a detailed understanding of what the current contractor management practices were and what the ideal state would be for their various constituencies.

Once the desired state was agreed on and the risks to achieving it were well understood, Rio Tinto went about the task of building a business unit–specific business case. This effort looked at both "nonfinancial benefits" (health/safety/efficiency) and financial measures (net present value analysis). To begin the process of quantifying the nonfinancial benefits, Rio Tinto held a Value Mapping workshop, based on the results of its To Be State workshop.

The results of these workshops detailed the benefits from a nonfinancial perspective. The conclusion was that the benefits that would flow from a fundamental change to the way that Rio Tinto manages contractors would be substantial. Contractors' health and safety would improve through increased control over their service providers by ensuring that they are prequalified for the work they are doing. The approach created more transparency and traceability of induction, qualification, and training records; resulted in better confirmation and tracking of medical records; and increased their ability to define the work that needs to be done. It also heightened management's

(Continued)

visibility of which contractors are on site, how long they have been working on site, and the type of work they are doing. Finally, it created a clear linkage between being in compliance with the company's health and safety standards and site access.

In summary, the following nine tasks were completed during stage 2 (planning):

1. Developed a project plan.
2. Held To Be State workshop.
3. Developed a business unit business case.
4. Conducted risk assessment.
5. Developed a change management plan.
6. Defined the business process and business rules.
7. Identified technology configuration needs.
8. Migrated data from legacy systems.
9. Created a requirements document.

In stage 3 (execution and compliance), Rio Tinto put its plan into action by first holding a series of communication meetings with managers, suppliers, and employees. These were designed to share the business need, the vision for the future, and the business case. Rio Tinto's next action was to provide training tailored to each of these constituencies, detailing exactly what needed to be done to bring contract labor on board.

Rio Tinto set up and staffed an on-site program office to provide and establish an infrastructure that supported the development of rate cards, invoicing forms, and reports. This was all done using a "high touch" approach that gave management instant access to the MSP and technical resources to make sure questions or issues that needed to be addressed were quickly resolved. To ensure a successful "go live" for the system, Rio Tinto piloted the system with a limited number of suppliers and did extensive user acceptance testing.

In summary, the following tasks were completed during stage 3 (execution and compliance):

1. Launched business unit communication plan.
2. Customized training for all users of the CMS (i.e., managers, suppliers, and employees).
3. Put a program office in place.
4. Developed rate cards, invoicing, and reports.
5. VMS initiated a pilot with user acceptance testing prior to switchover.

6. Evaluated the pilot before "go live."

7. Communicated "go live," training, and program launch.

8. Performed a data audit.

9. Gathered user feedback.

10. Documented lessons learned.

11. Prepared a compliance review.

In stage 4 (transition to operations), Rio Tinto conducted

1. A business review;

2. A client/supplier satisfaction survey; and finally

3. A moved from implementation to operations.

The business review looked at the degree to which Rio Tinto had achieved the goals, both in the area of health and safety, and from a financial perspective. Rio Tinto significantly increased the number of contractors who were properly prequalified, mobilized, medically validated, and inducted from 55 to 98 percent. The new system clearly demonstrated to its suppliers the linkage between being in compliance with the company's health, safety and environmental policies and having site access. The new contractor management process provided leadership with access to real-time accurate information on contractor status and costs for the first time (see sample dashboard in Exhibit 2.7). Users reported greater satisfaction with the new process (the percentage of users who said they were satisfied increased from 48 to 81 percent) and reported 11 percent less time spent doing administrative work. This increased the amount of time they could spend in direct supervision of contractors, which they believe will also have a positive impact on safety. Rio Tinto was also able to reduce the number of outstanding invoices and move to 100 percent compliance with the new contractor management procedures. In addition, Rio Tinto was able to track cost savings of around 5 percent, derived from competitiveness, negotiation, and usage efficiency.

After 12 months of using the contractor management system, business management felt that it was a success:

Implementation of the contractor management solution at ERA is a "good news story"; the solution is going to save us a lot of money— no doubt.

—Chief executive of the pilot site

(Continued)

Metric		Baseline	Interim	Project	Measurement Method
Short Title	Detail	Jan 2011	May 2011	Target	
HS&E Improvements	Number of contractors properly prequalified, mobilized, and inducted	48%	86%	100%	Random selection of 10% of contractors in system to be audited
Transparency	Leadership access to real-time, accurate information of contractor status and costs	47%	90%	100%	Survey to be conducted with key users, DMs, vendors, and management
User Satisfaction	Approach to contractor administration under the existing self-service model vs. the new consolidated model	80%	85%	85%	Survey to be conducted with key users, DMs, vendors, and management
Improved Efficiency	Percentage of work time spent by designated managers in contractor administration activities	32% DM 16% V	31% DM 14% V	Reduction of 40% (20%)	Survey to be conducted with key users and DMs
Reduced Outstanding Invoices	Overdue invoices for engaged vendors before vs. vendors after	52 (11)	10	Zero	AP Web cycle report before and after for included vendors
Process Compliance	% of designated managers using the new system	–	TBC	100% of pilot	Measurement of PRs raised for contractor works where vendors are on the system
Rate Compliance	Contracted rates vs. actual rates	Outstanding analysis	Outstanding analysis	100% invoicing at contracted rates	Random selection of 10% of contractors in system to be audited

Exhibit 2.7 Implementation
Reprinted with permission from Rio Tinto

The solution is starting to give me better visibility of what's going on with contractors in the operation, and this level of control is extremely important for someone in my position.

—General manager of operations

Since the VMS I have placed the majority of the contractors in this system, which has *given me back about two days of time* (a week), as I don't have to do inductions, medical sign-offs. I don't have to complete about 60 service entries a week, and with VMS, 60 time sheets can be checked and approved in less than a minute.

—Maintenance supervisor

Once the system was up and running, Rio Tinto audited the data in the system to ensure that information was being captured correctly and that the system was working from end-to-end. Rio Tinto then solicited feedback from end users, holding a series of workshops to extract the lessons learned.

Major Lessons Learned

There were a number of lessons learned in how to manage change in a business:

- Ensure that the data analysis leads to the identification of the root cause of the problem with face validity.
- Select an issue that is a core driver for the company and is consistent with culture and values.
- Work cross-functionally to create synergy and ensure full support for solution development and implementation.
- Design the solution in conjunction with the business to ensure adoption and minimize resistance.
- Adequately resource the project at every level, from conception to final review and implementation.

The best endorsement is that Rio Tinto's contractor management system has been adopted as a global standard and is being deployed around the world.

SUMMARY

This chapter has mapped out the basics of what alignment is and why it is necessary. You should have an idea of who should be involved, as well as what the alignment discussions will include and accomplish. Chapter 3 will explore the details of creating a measurement plan (another goal of the stakeholder meeting). Gathering the stakeholders and gaining their agreement on the goals of an investment is not an easy, straightforward process. However, it has lasting benefits to the investment and the organization as a whole.

The alignment process is useful all on its own, independent of the measurement project. Aligning stakeholders on the definition of success is a useful and valuable process for just about any type of investment in people and can benefit almost any size organization. It will help HR be a better strategic business partner. It also ensures that HR is practicing fiscal responsibility with its often-limited budget. The alignment process is also useful in high-level planning, before an investment has even been identified. Perhaps the business has given you a goal or a business problem to solve. Tap your stakeholders and align with them on how to achieve the goal. Not only are they likely to have great ideas, but they will also appreciate your request for their input, and you will build better business partnerships for the long run.

NOTES

1. S. Anthony, M. Johnson, J. Sinfield, and E. Altman, *An Innovator's Guide to Growth: Putting Disruptive Innovation to Work* (Boston: Harvard Business School Press, 2008), 247.
2. L. Bassie, E. Frauenheim, D. McMurrer, and L. Costello, *Good Company: Business Success in the Worthiness Era* (San Francisco: Berrett-Koehler, 2011).
3. D. L. Cooperrider, "Introduction to Appreciative Inquiry," in W. French and C. Bell, *Organization Development: Behavioral Science Interventions for Organization Improvemet*, 5th ed. (Englewood Cliffs, NJ: Prentice Hall, 1995).
4. D. Hubbard, *How to Measure Anything: Finding the Value of "Intangibles" in Business* (Hoboken, NJ: John Wiley & Sons, 2007).
5. J. R. French, "Field Experiments: Changing Group Productivity," in J. Miller, *Experiments in Social Process: A Symposium on Social Psychology* (New York: McGraw-Hill, 1950), 52.
6. C. Jones, O. Bonsignour, and J. Subramanyam, *The Economics of Software Quality* (Boston: Addison-Wesley Longman, 2011).

CHAPTER **3**

The Measurement Plan

"Measurement always improves performance."
—Marcus Buckingham and Curt Coffman[1]

Once you have completed the process of alignment with your stakeholders, you are ready to put together an action plan for measuring your investment. A good measurement plan will include the following components:

- Definition of the intervention or interventions to be studied
- Measurement map
- Business questions or hypotheses
- Metrics
- Demographics
- Data sources and requirements
- Participant and nonparticipant groups
- Internal and external variables affecting performance
- Project plan with major milestones
- Personnel required to manage the study
- Communication plan for results

A good practice is to pull together your measurement plan directly following the stakeholder meeting and offer to review it with any interested stakeholders.

DEFINING THE INTERVENTION(S)

This part should be relatively easy and is likely something you can do prior to the stakeholder meeting. If your study includes a group of interventions, be sure to clearly define what is and is not included. You may also want to consider selecting a subset of interventions that is representative of a larger program. We worked with a large government agency that wanted to evaluate the impact of hundreds of courses offered to employees for continuing education. We collaborated with the stakeholders and created a process to select a sample of courses that represented the larger investment. Criteria included such factors as number of course completions, knowledge transfer by course (as determined by pre- and post-test scores), and survey results (did participants like the course and think it was valuable?). If you are using this technique, make sure the representative sample is large enough to truly represent the investment in its entirety but also limited enough to make the measurement study manageable.

In defining the intervention for your measurement plan, include the following details:

- Name of the intervention(s) and selected components to be included in the evaluation (if applicable).
- Number of participants who received the intervention.
- Number of participants who did not receive the intervention.
- Intervention deployment plan including start date and target completion date.
- Details of process by which participants were selected to receive the intervention. If HR or another department did not select the participants, was there a self-selection process at work?
- Total cost of the intervention—measured in terms of fixed costs overall or a variable cost per participant.

MEASUREMENT MAP

A measurement map is a visual depiction of the alignment between an investment and the organization's strategic goals. By showing the logical relationships between the investment and goals, the map provides the measurable links that form the basis of your study. You will create this map as you go through the process of identifying goals, business results, and leading indicators with your stakeholders. In order to establish causality and analyze impact, the links must be measurable.

In the context of the measurement map, we use these definitions:

- **Investments in people.** This is the intervention or series of interventions intended to drive business results. It can be any type of investment in human capital—a training event, a recognition program, a performance management process, and so on.

- **Leading indicators.** Leading indicators are nonfinancial values that suggest whether you are on the right track. They appear early in the causal chain and provide early evidence of measurable business outcomes. See Chapter 2 for a more detailed discussion and examples of leading indicators.

- **Business results.** Often referred to as key performance indicators (KPIs), business impact metrics are tied to a financial value. If a metric does not have a financial value, it is not a business impact metric. See Chapter 2 for examples of business impact metrics.

- **Strategic goals.** The desired end results of the initiative or set of initiatives. For most organizations, this ultimately boils down to improving financial performance—either by increasing revenue or decreasing costs.

Frequently, both the investment and the strategic goal are known, but the links have not been clearly defined. Sometimes the end game is known, but the investment has yet to be determined. So the map helps clarify the objectives and expected outcomes, thereby helping to shape the investment.

Exhibit 3.1 shows a measurement map for a sales training initiative.

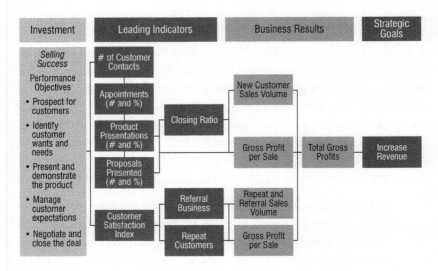

Exhibit 3.1 Measurement Map

Notice that there are multiple layers of leading indicators and business results. In this case, Contacts, Appointments, Presentations, and Proposals are all leading indicators for the Closing Ratio. The Closing Ratio, in turn, is linked to the business results New Customer Sales Volume and Gross Profit per Sale. Both of these indicators link to financial value, as well as to another business result: Total Gross Profits. These leading indicators and business results are arranged to show the logical links between the performance objectives of the sales training program and the strategic goal of increasing revenue.

Sales training is a good demonstration of the map, due to its rather straightforward links to the strategic goal. Because the links are closely tied to the organization's specific investment and structure, no two maps will look alike. A measurement map can also be used when the investment has been made but the expected outcomes remain vague. Just like a road map or a flow chart, a measurement map can be read from either end—starting with the point of origin (the investment) to the destination (strategic goals) or vice versa.

Consider the example of a leadership development investment. A leadership development initiative is often difficult to measure due to its typical nonmeasurable objectives (develop leadership capabilities, improve company culture, and so on). For example, the logic of the measurement map could propose that if the program's objectives are met, they should manifest in the leaders' performance in four key ways:

1. Creating development plans.
2. Conducting mid-year and annual reviews for direct reports.
3. Sending staff to skill-building training.
4. Taking advantage of the company's recognition program.

These are examples of leading indicators, all of which should produce data within the organization. If those leading indicators show positive results, it follows that employees (leaders and associates) will have promotional and cross-functional opportunities, engagement scores will increase, and the pipeline of next-generation leaders will begin to fill.

The majority of organizations have this type of data. All of these leading indicators point to business results where outcomes can be quantified in dollars. Increased retention reduces the costs associated with turnover. Increased internal hire rates reduce the expenses of recruiting and onboarding. Both lead to reduced costs, which translate to improved financial performance.

These simple examples illustrate how a measurement map guides the deconstruction of the investment down to observable, on-the-job behaviors that the organization desires. If the leading indicators are improving, the map indicates that business results will also improve, ultimately driving toward the strategic goal.

In order to create a measurement map, you will draw on the expertise of your stakeholders. In Chapter 2, we talked about aligning stakeholders with the goals for an investment; this is also the first step to creating a measurement map. (Please note that this map begins with the investment—a map that begins with the strategic goal and that is used to come up with an investment to drive that goal will follow a slightly different process.)

The key, as stressed in Chapter 2, is to momentarily set aside questions about metrics and data sources. One of the beautiful things about the map is that it provides multiple leading indicators and business results. We encourage you to include as many of these indicators as possible in your map, whether or not the underlying data are available. By identifying and prioritizing key measures early in the process, you can begin new data collection initiatives based on the map.

Start with open-ended questions, such as

- What should people be able to do after participating in this program?
- What would be different because of the program?
- What would be evidence of that difference?
- How do we measure that?

As you follow this line of thinking, it is important to make sure that all of the key performance indicators (KPIs) on the map are measurable. Nonmeasurable goals may be tracked anecdotally but will not be part of the map.

The process of creating a measurement map is an art, not a science. No two will look alike (even if they are for the same investment in different organizations). The point of the mapping process is to illustrate alignment and create a common language around what to measure. If your map achieves that goal, it works.

HYPOTHESES OR BUSINESS QUESTIONS

The business hypotheses for the study are decided on in collaboration with your stakeholders (see Chapter 2 for a deeper discussion). Although they can cover a range of topics, it is essential that they have a definitive, quantifiable answer. For example, stakeholders may want to know, "Does our leadership development program produce better leaders?" This is not a question you can prove or disprove with data. However, if you refer back to your measurement map, you will find the business results you selected as relevant to the leadership development program. "Does our leadership development program have a positive impact on leader and subordinate retention?" is a question that can be definitively answered with data.

DEFINING THE METRICS

Finally, we come to the metrics—the place where most HR practitioners want to start. While we agree that metrics are very important, we would like to offer a caution: just because a metric exists, that does not necessarily mean it should have a place of importance in your study. Measurement is an activity, and activity is expense. So, only measure something that adds value through revenue growth or expense reduction.

A metric is something that can be quantified to describe the outcome of a business process. The measurement map's leading indicators and business results will typically map to existing metrics. If there are points on the map that do not correspond to existing metrics (it is relatively common for a few leading indicators to be things that the organization is not currently measuring), you have a couple of options. First, you can start collecting the necessary data. However, because you may need performance data for a period preceding the investment, a new metric may not be feasible.

Another option is to identify surrogate metrics. These are existing metrics that help to quantify an otherwise nonmeasurable link in the causal chain. For example, say you want to measure the impact of a mentoring program, but the employees participating in the program are knowledge workers whose performance is not specifically quantified. Think about other indicators of performance—annual review scores, bonuses, stock grants, and merit pay are four surrogate metrics that could stand in for employee performance in this case.

As you are mapping links in the measurement map to metrics, also remember to consider a wide variety of data sources. Many of the metrics in your HR system will be useful, but you will also want to include metrics from other areas of the business that are affected by the investment. For example, if the goal of a leadership program is to improve plant safety scores, you will need to work with your stakeholders from operations to gain access to safety metrics. Remember to also do a gut check on the validity and utility of a metric. The point is to ensure that your selected metrics is indeed a valid and useful measure of performance. This is discussed in more detail in Chapter 4. Another common problem is to identify the most important metrics, regardless of whether the intervention has anything to do with them. We saw one project that ended with soured expectations when the company's most important metric, major equipment repairs, was not affected by participation in a customer relationship training program.

For the measurement plan, create a basic list of information about each metric. There may be several different versions of each metric—for example, sales could be measured in units, gross dollars, or net profits. Here is a checklist of what you should know about each metric:

- Name of the metric.
- Units in which the metric is measured (hours, dollars, percentage points, etc.).
- Maximum and minimum range of the metric (in some cases, negative values are not permissible).
- Dates for which the data are available (is information available both before and after the investment?).
- Unit financial value (how much is it worth?).
- Desired direction of change (increase or decrease).
- Expected impact of the investment.
- Contact: Who is in charge of collecting this metric? Who can answer questions about it?

It may take time to collect all the information required. Defining costs, in particular, may present a significant challenge when you are trying to find agreement among multiple stakeholders. If you are not able to secure cost metrics until quite late in the project, do not exclude it as a metric. If you focus on other data collection and analysis, the cost estimates can be the financial icing on the cake.

DEMOGRAPHICS

As you create the measurement plan, consider which demographics have a reasonable connection to the investment, as well as the type of demographic data that is available. Later chapters of this book explain how to segment impact findings by demographic groups to show you where—and with whom—the investment is or is not working.

We identify two categories of demographics: individual and organizational. Individual demographics are what most people think of when they hear the term *demographics*. They describe an individual's personal traits, such as gender, age, education level, ethnicity, and so on. Organizational demographics are derived from some unit the individual is part of, for example, region, division, work unit, and so forth. These data come from a different source and are linked back to the individual. It is important to include both types of demographics, because both can affect how an individual responds to an investment.

The majority of individual demographics remain stable over time (education level is one exception). The organizational demographics can be more fluid, which presents a data challenge. Say you want to include performance of a manager's direct reports in a leadership development study. Many HR systems will tell you to whom an individual currently reports but will not include historical data on the manager-subordinate relationship. You will need to come up with another way to determine how long the individual has reported to the manager and whether a manager's direct reports changed during the course of the study. This is a good example of where surveys can help fill in missing data.

There are two important considerations when selecting the demographics to include in the measurement plan. First, can an individual's demographic have an impact on his or her performance, as measured by one or more metrics? Second, can the individual's demographic predict the impact of the investment? If you can get the individual's shoe size, it seems unlikely to provide you with much usefulness in the analysis. Demographics typically remain constant throughout the study (items such as "age" and "tenure" are usually fixed as of one date).

Here is a checklist of information your measurement plan should include for each demographic:

- Description.
- Unit of measure (categorical, continuous numeric, true/false).

- Minimum and maximum possible values (for numeric).
- Number and list of valid categories (for categorical).
- Distribution of participants across categories (for categorical).
- Categories of ranges (for example, age could be grouped into categories).
- Contact or expert within the organization who can take responsibility for answering questions.

DATA SOURCES AND REQUIREMENTS

Once the metrics and demographics for the study have been established, you are ready to tackle the data sources and requirements. This is another area to rely on your stakeholders, as well as on the individuals within their departments who administer data. The stakeholders will be able to tell you where data live, but you will want to interact with the analysts to get details about the data and make sure you are requesting what you need.

CASE STUDY

SUN MICROSYSTEMS

Background

Sun Microsystems has developed computer servers, workstations, storage systems, and more in support of open systems and open source software. The vision of Sun Microsystems was "the network is the computer"—a collaborative network participation through shared innovation, community development, and open source leadership. This vision extends to organizational learning. Sun has become a thought leader in the evolution from "push" learning paradigms to a "pull" model. In comparison to Learning 1.0 models of scheduled learning events, Learning 2.0 embraces a more informal and collaborative approach with user-created content at its core. In August 2008, Sun Learning Services (SLS) launched Social Learning eXchange (SLX), an applied and successful real-world example of this vision.

Intervention: Social Learning Xchange

SLX is a learning portal that Karie Willyerd, VP and Chief Learning Officer, described as "YouTube meets iTunes." The portal supports user-generated content, cloud tags, broad search capabilities, and a social network of experts. The early results were encouraging. Within the first 4 weeks, usage doubled and exceeded the 10-week adoption goal.

SLX is presented as a tool for use in four broad arenas: sales, collaboration, corporate communications, and learning. Such a broad set of uses demanded that measurement map a variety of metrics to diverse business processes.

Measurement Design

The business impact study focused on the use of SLX as a learning modality compared to instructor-led training (ILT) and web-based training (WBT). Prior to the launch of SLX, Sun recorded more than six million hours of formal training between July 2007 and June 2008. The analysis calculated the return on investment (ROI) of SLX. The goals of SLX were ambitious and far-reaching, so the measurement project had to consider performance, savings, usage, and many other factors. Because the population using the system was diverse, it was not possible to track some types of usage, and because of the broad goals, the measurement plan needed to be mindful of where the opportunities for measurement presented themselves. Four research questions directed the analysis:

1. Does SLX increase the portfolio of content at the same or lower cost than previous methods?
2. Does SLX reach more unique users at the same or lower cost than the existing cost per user?
3. Does SLX allow for more efficient use of subject matter experts (SMEs) and content developers at the same or lower cost than previous techniques?
4. Does SLX reduce the time to develop and deliver content in comparison to previous systems?

In addition to a positive ROI, SLX was intended to create value by:

- Enabling informal, social learning with a platform that mirrors popular social networking trends and empowers SMEs and others to easily capture and interactively share knowledge.

(Continued)

- Improving return on training dollars by reducing or eliminating costly ILT and enabling the rapid creation of blended learning solutions.
- Making training and learning more efficient as SMEs and learning professionals alike quickly author and publish content, and learners access relevant, compelling, peer-to-peer, and formal training materials when they need them.
- Increasing learning speed for everyone, from new employees to sales reps, specialists, and enterprise partners, with engaging content available 24/7.
- Enabling employees to access content from the field using mobile devices.

The data were gathered from several sources and perspectives, including SLX usage information, operating information from SLS about development costs and resource requirements, and qualitative interviews with SMEs, SLX developers, and key users. This project differed from many, because it was more difficult to determine who the user was, and also because users came from literally every time of job and role within Sun. This put the focus on metrics that related to the usage of the system. Because there was no incentive or pressure to use or rate content in any particular way, we could make stronger assumptions about the popularity of content equating with usefulness. The usage was considered not just from the perspective of the end user but also from a production viewpoint: How much content was created to fill the role of expensive materials created for the classroom or traditional WBT?

Quantitative Analysis

The business impact study evaluated Sun's entire learning investments between July 2007 and June 2009. It detailed the number of learning titles, enrollments, and content development time. SLX data were available from implementation through November 2009. More than 4,800 unique titles were created during this period (traditional ILT and WBT plus SLX titles). These initiated more than 37,600 instructor-led enrollments, 756,000 web-based enrollments, and 115,700 SLX views.

Qualitative Analysis

Six senior managers were also interviewed about their experiences with SLX as a learning and communications tool. Additionally, both internal and third party assessments of SLX were conducted; findings were submitted for review by the learning industry.

Business Impact

SLX positively impacted Sun's learning environment in numerous ways (see Exhibit 3.2). The system provided more diverse content. SLX was directly responsible for the creation and delivery of 3,982 titles. Interviews and anecdotal evidence indicate this modality was an extremely efficient use of SMEs' and content developers' time. Additionally, SLX enabled near instantaneous deployment of critical training titles versus the time required for traditional course development. Comparing development and delivery costs of traditional WBT to those associated with SLX, SLX provided Sun with a benefit-to-cost ratio of 75:1, representing a net benefit of $25.9 million.

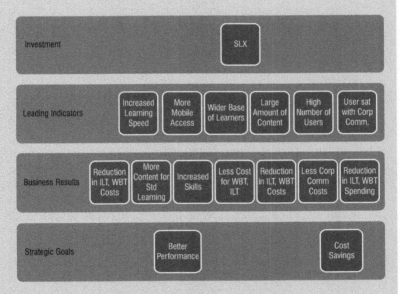

Exhibit 3.2   A Measurement Map of the Sun SLX Study
Reprinted with permission from Sun Microsystems

Key Findings

The findings are presented in three views: usage of SLX, investment in SLX, and quality of SLX content.

(Continued)

Usage

From full launch in August 2008 through November 2009, nearly 11,000 active employees accessed SLX content at least once, representing nearly 40 percent of Sun's workforce.

In total:

- 3,982 unique SLX titles were created
- 21,364 hours of content were viewed
- There were 168,495 views (multiple views per day per user excluded)
- The average usage per user was 45 minutes per month

The use of SLX was widespread. The application was developed first as a sales support tool, so it is not surprising that Global Sales and Services represented over 76 percent of all content views. Proportionately, this group and Corporate Resources viewed more hours of content than they created. Application Platform Software generated 45 percent of all content hours created.

Investment

Although ILT requires less investment for development, the delivery costs are high. The average total cost per hour delivered for the two-year period was $292.

Formal WBT with full interactive features requires more development time. WBT averages 200 hours of development for every hour of final content. However, it has low delivery costs and allows for faster deployment. WBT is also well suited for international delivery. The average total cost per hour delivered for WBT was $83, including $5 for delivery, which is 70 percent less than ILT.

SLX is a web-based application with the same infrastructure requirements as WBT. The delivery cost of $5 per hour is the same for both. The differences between the two are development time and labor costs. The screen capture features of SLX and the ease of uploading file types created in other desktop applications reduce the average development time to two hours for every hour of content. Additionally, traditional instructional design and content development expertise is not necessary in the SLX environment. Sun determined this represented a 28 percent reduction in the development rate used in cost calculations.

To calculate the ROI, it is assumed that all SLX content was developed and delivered through WBT. The premise of SLX is to deliver shorter and timelier content when the content allows. The ROI was calculated by applying the traditional WBT development hours and rates to the SLX content. These calculations revealed an ROI of 7,505 percent. Put another way, every $1 invested in SLX reduced the need to invest in WBT by $75. Assuming the full cost of the software development investment is expensed in the first year, the net benefit was $25.9 million.

Content Quality

By design, the majority of content uploaded to SLX is user-generated, informal, and shorter. In fact, the average length of SLX content is 36 minutes compared to 1.5 hours for WBT and 2.5 hours for ILT. The informal, shorter nature of this new content raised the question of quality and utility. Based on usage, content ratings, and other feedback, Sun determined that the platform did provide quality and utility.

Exhibit 3.3 illustrates the percentage of content that was rated, embedded, and/or downloaded by users. Many pieces of content were downloaded and rated, downloaded and embedded, and so on. Of note, only 14 percent of this user-created content was not viewed (creators were excluded as users of their own content).

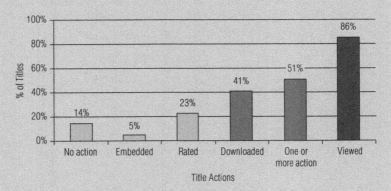

Exhibit 3.3 Interest in SLX Content from January 2008 to December 2009
Reprinted with permission from Sun Microsystems

- **No action.** A title was uploaded, but there were no corresponding views or other actions.
- **Embedded.** These were media titles where the recipient embedded the URL into another web page. The assumption is that the individual deemed it valuable enough to endorse and share. A distant and conscious effort is required.

(Continued)

- **Rated.** The media was rated using a scoring systems of 1 to 5 stars. A distinct and conscious effort is required.
- **Downloaded.** The media was downloaded to one or more devices by an individual. The working assumption is that all titles that are downloaded are eventually viewed.
- **One or more actions.** Fifty-one percent of the titles had some combination of rating, downloading, or embedding.
- **Viewed.** Eighty-six percent of all titles were viewed (this includes the 51 percent where users took action beyond simply viewing).

Users rated 23 percent of the content with a standard "star rating" system (1 to 5 stars). The average rating per title was 4.25 stars. Consistent usage also suggests high utility value of SLX's user-created content. Titles remained active—in some cases for as long as 12 months. Titles were viewed on average 41 times. Following a pilot, usage rose dramatically after the third quarter 2008 launch and has remained at high levels, indicating user acceptance of this new delivery platform.

Exhibit 3.4 shows the trend of hours viewed by quarter. If the content specifically or SLX in general were not useful, it was expected that ratings, views, and content contributions would all decline. This was not the case.

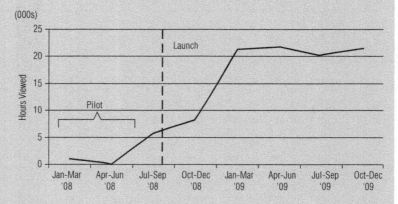

Exhibit 3.4 Total SLX Hours Viewed
Reprinted with permission from Sun Microsystems

Implications

Sun's experience is an invaluable example of the potential for informal learning and structured use of social media. By leveraging its culture and technical expertise, Sun Learning Services created an agile and relevant training environment. Pull models are particularly effective with adult learners. Accessing the right information at the time that it is needed almost guarantees retention and application. And the fact that it can be accomplished with a positive ROI is extremely compelling.

SUMMARY

Once you have completed the process of alignment with your stakeholders, you are ready to put together an action plan for measuring your investment. A good practice is to pull together your measurement plan directly following the stakeholder meeting and offer to review it with any interested stakeholders. If your study includes a group of interventions, be sure to clearly define what is and is not included. You may also want to consider selecting a subset of interventions that is representative of a larger program.

A measurement map is a visual depiction of the alignment between an investment and the organization's strategic goals. The map provides the measurable links that form the basis of your study by using business metrics to show the logical relationships between the investment and goals. A metric is something that can be quantified to describe the outcome of a business process. Demographic data is an important source for metrics. The measurement map's leading indicators and business results will typically map to your metrics. Once the metrics and the demographics for the study have been established, you are ready to tackle the data sources and requirements.

NOTE

1. M. Buckingham and C. Coffman, *First, Break All the Rules* (New York: Simon & Schuster, 1999).

CHAPTER **4**

It's All about the Data

"In God we trust; all others must bring data."

—W. Edwards Deming[1]

W hen many of the theories and paradigms that govern measurement were developed, computer size was measured in kilobytes, rather than gigabytes. When Kirkpatrick was laying out his famous four levels of measurement and NASA was launching the Apollo missions, IBM's high-end computers had only 8M of memory.[2] Compare that to your smartphone today. Advances in technology and increases in computing power have brought with them an unprecedented avalanche of data. The problem now is to find the needle you want in the haystack of data, cultivate the expertise and the political will to gain access to data, tie them together, and extract useful intelligence. Data are the very core of your analytics initiative. Do you have the information you need? How do you handle it when you get it? What if you can't find what you were looking for? What issues surround the politics, the ethics, and the strategy?

For a successful measurement initiative, you will want to draw data from two or three, or perhaps more, major sources around the organization. The type of data you need comes out of the alignment process. Your stakeholders and measurement plan will help you identify the appropriate sources. Here are some common examples:

- Operations
- Compensation
- Customer service
- Human resources information systems (HRIS)
- Learning management systems (LMS)
- Social media and nontraditional learning systems
- Engagement
- Surveys
- Performance management systems
- Interviews and estimation by experts
- Public data from outside the organization

For each source of data, it is important to know where the data are housed, who the owner is, how you will collaborate with the owner, how you will obtain and integrate the information with other data, and ultimately, how valid and reliable it is. In the next section, we will describe each type in turn.

TYPES OF DATA

Operational data tracks the business processes within the organization. It might be revenue or sales commissions, information from within a call center, defect information from an assembly line, safety incident logs, or many other things. This type of data is probably the most difficult for us to discuss, because it varies so widely across organizations. Operational data has the advantage that it is closest to the cash flow of the enterprise and is thus likely to be well-organized and closely tracked. Unlike human resource data, operational data is not usually tied to personal privacy issues and constraints. Unlike survey data, operational data is not subject to an employee's willingness to fill out a survey accurately and is more objective. When operational data is analyzed, the results usually have instant credibility because the metrics align with those tracked by executives. If a metric you consider important is not being tracked, there are two possible reasons: either you are mistaken in your assessment of its importance, or the organization is not collecting the data it needs to manage operations. Either reason requires careful reflection before proceeding.

Customer service data addresses important business processes, particularly in organizations where there is a high ratio of customer-facing employees, or "surface area." Customer service can be measured in many ways, both with leading indicators (such as reported satisfaction) or as business results with more direct costs (such as number of items returned). The lines between different classes of metrics may be a bit blurry, because number of items returned could be perceived as a leading indicator of customer satisfaction, quality, or directly as an operational metric that costs the company money for each item returned.

Human resource information systems (HRIS) are an important part of most projects. Primarily, they provide demographic information, such as education, tenure, job title, and other items. Sometimes HRIS systems contain other types of data, such as compensation data. In most cases, human resources data provides the master list of participants in the measurement project and is the most likely source for mapping data that ties different data sets together (e.g., the employee name, ID, and e-mail address might all be here, but only one may be recorded in other data).

Learning management systems (LMS) contain information about training, which is a common focus of human capital investment measurements. The LMS may contain some way of identifying the employee, the type of training they received, and the date on which they received the training. LMS systems for online training virtually always contain ways of tracking this information. For organizations using traditional classroom methods, some dedicated system may contain the bookings for classroom learning. It's also possible that the data may be just a spreadsheet on someone's desktop. Learning data is usually easy to obtain; the only real danger is that learning systems have their own log-ins that do not always match up with e-mail addresses or employee IDs in other systems.

Social media and informal learning systems are becoming more and more important. Organizations are using social media in several fashions:

- Promoting or sharing information about the company with outsiders, such as having a Facebook page, a Twitter account, or offering coupons through Groupon.

- Passively measuring and recording public sentiment about the company or products to set policy (e.g., an auto company noting that customers were complaining about the quality of the paint job on an auto shopping network).

- Using social media tools internally, such as providing a forum for employees to browse and post useful content, to partially or fully replace traditional learning systems, or to communicate among employees.

The mind-set of social media is a major challenge for many organizations, because it requires relinquishing central control and allowing free, unstructured exchange of information. Internal social media systems can provide some basic information, at least at what you can call Kirkpatrick level 0 or 1: usage and popularity.[3] (See Appendix A for more information about Kirkpatrick levels.) If information is collected that allows you to figure out who is using the content, it is possible to directly measure impact on individuals. External social media systems may be difficult or impossible platforms on which to measure information. The system administrators at your organization may be able to identify where the traffic is going but probably not much else.

Engagement surveys are effective instruments for gauging sentiment by employees and are gaining popularity. The questions may be viewed individually ("I have a best friend at work") or aggregated into various subsets, gauging employees' satisfaction with their manager or their view of career prospects. Because of confidentiality concerns, engagement surveys are sometimes difficult to map directly to particular employees or even to particular managers or divisions. This is an area where a third-party service may prove useful. The idea is that engagement surveys are best if they are confidential but not completely anonymous. If the employees can write without being worried about who might read their information, the goal is served. For more detailed information on engagement and how it can be linked to business outcomes, see the Lowe's case study in Chapter 1.

Psychological testing shows promise in predicting performance on job metrics, both in an individual sense and in how individuals fit together in a team.[4] The role of "psychological and social capital" in creating and maintaining a dynamic, productive workplace is an area of growing importance. Some respected research suggests that concepts such as self-efficacy, hope, and resilience are important constructs in understanding employee performance.[5] Research in how to apply this work within the organization is growing but has not been developed into a well-understood practice with common usage.

Survey data can take in quite a wide range of information and can provide data in many different categories. Some popular uses for surveys include

- Customer satisfaction
- Trainee satisfaction with course materials
- Engagement data

There are a few important caveats about surveys. First, surveys are one of those things that seem easy to do but are quite difficult to do correctly. Confidentiality and social pressure can heavily bias results in a survey, based on what participants think they should answer, or who they think might read it. Fairly minor changes in wording can drive large changes in estimation. For example, one experiment asked participants about a film of an automobile accident they had seen. The answers varied, based on the verbs used to describe the collision: when asked to estimate the speed, the difference between "contacted" and "smashed" was nine miles per hour.[6] Finally, response rates on surveys are often low. People who fill them out may differ greatly from those who do not.

There is an excellent story about surveys from the book *Freakonomics* that drives home how perilous surveys can be, the importance of question design, and the ways monetary and other issues manipulate how honest respondents are.[7] Have you heard of the night seven million American children disappeared? April 14, 1987? The children vanished due to a change in a survey question. The Internal Revenue Service gives a moderate tax break based on the number of dependents (children). The American "1040" standard tax form used to ask the question, "How many dependents do you have?" In 1987, the question was changed to "List the names and social security numbers of your dependents." When the more rigorous question was asked, taxpayers perceived that providing social security numbers would allow their answers to be checked and penalties assessed on the dishonest. Consequently, the number showed a radical drop from the previous year. The results of this seemingly innocuous change highlight the importance of carefully worded survey questions and illustrate how concerns such as money, social pressure, and prosecution can sway results.

Surveys are excellent ways to make short-term, tactical decisions about training courses. Although we prefer more rigorous tools to isolate impact, there are numerous tasks best suited to surveys. Some examples include

- Finding course materials that are most and least popular with students.
- Determining whether pacing is appropriate.
- Judging individual instructor style and quality.

Note that these types of findings are highly relevant for the designers of the training, although of lesser interest outside of the learning and development group. Surveys have been used as a direct method of assessing ROI by many excellent practitioners, although we prefer operational data as our first option.[8]

Performance management systems include internal rating and planning systems designed to evaluate employees or teams or to plan for future development for those employees. Some examples include 360 programs, where the employee is evaluated by managers, subordinates, and peers; various systems where the employee explicitly sets goals and strategy for the coming year; and simple manager rating systems. Measurement and evaluation efforts have some interesting relationships within these systems. First, the outputs of such a system can be viewed as the key performance indicator, which enables questions about the relationships between investments and employee performance. For example, does the new leadership development program result in more highly rated employees? Prior-year ratings may also show a strong selection bias in who receives training or other special programs, either positively (high scoring, well-regarded employees are rewarded) or negatively (low performers and those on probation may be singled out for remedial action). The relationship between ratings in a performance system and other KPIs can be tested, which serves as a validity check on the performance management system. For example, "Did those who made good plans or who were rated highly differ in important ways?" "Were they more likely to stay, be promoted, sell more units, or have more engaged subordinates?"

In one interesting project, we had the opportunity to be a part of implementing a new performance management process for a major apparel manufacturer, VF. This project is described in further detail in a case study in a later chapter. The organization included systematic measurement and evaluation in the implementation process. We helped rate the plans using the SMART (Specific, Measurable, Actionable, Relevant, Timely) criteria and provided insights and feedback on how employees were executing the new process.[9] Further analytics helped locate opportunities for improving participation and compliance. We were able to isolate factors that predicted employee participation. Although business unit and job role were indicators, the manager's participation was the single most important factor predicting subordinate participation. For more details, see the VF case study in Chapter 5.

Expert estimation is one way of collecting data about many things. For some future planning activities, it may be the best way available. Hubbard has done some excellent work in this area, with "Applied Information Economics." For areas such as IT risk assessment, this process focuses on how to get estimates to "fine-tune" the ability to identify a region with 90 or 95 percent comfort and certainty. For example, management might want to estimate the cost of a security breach, the likelihood of success for particular projects, or the amount of revenue a new product could generate. Expert estimation is most commonly applied to costs and risks. Yet because expert time is costly, it is seldom used to generate data on individual performance.

Finally, data generated entirely outside the organization may play a role in measurement. Occasionally, we use hiring or retention data from the Bureau of Labor Statistics. We have also used other sources to help us understand the relationship between data and time in an organization. For example, stock performance usually correlates positively with compensation and negatively with turnover. There are many industry-specific models to test the relationship between factory output and factors, such as commodity or fuel prices. Another area where external data have been relevant is the use of currency exchange rates to help make sense of monetary data in multinational companies.

Benchmarking is one major application of data from outside the organization. We generally are not fans of benchmarking. At best, it aspires to be like the competition. At worst, it suggests false goals. After dozens of measurement projects, we realize that understanding the data from within one organization can be quite challenging enough. A meta-analysis between organizations, assuming that you can use "sales revenue" or "turnover" in an apples-to-apples comparison, does not elicit confidence in the data. The difficulties of understanding one's own data are magnified by the number of organizations involved, the different time spans, the conventions under which they may be reporting, and their unwillingness to transparently share internal information with outside publishers. As noted by the Dilbert cartoon character, "If everyone is doing it, best practices is the same thing as mediocre."[10] Benchmarking does provide an important sanity check to see whether your own work is within the ballpark and helps "tell the story," because a natural question people ask is how they compare to others in their field. It provides invaluable background in setting the stage for a more rigorous study. In summary, benchmarking is a nice side dish but not the main course.

TYING YOUR DATA SETS TOGETHER

One of the most crucial tasks in an analysis is combining data from different sources for analysis. Database people talk about "unique identifiers"—a piece of information that can tie together data sources. Examples include social security numbers, e-mail addresses, and employee ID numbers. Note that there is exactly a one-to-one mapping between a person and each of these items, at least in theory. In practice, there may be data cleanup that needs to occur. For example, an e-mail address might be read by multiple people (e.g., sales@foo .com) or a company may issue a new employee IDs when someone transitions between full time and part time.

To make connections between data sets, your data analysts will need one or more unique identifiers. Sometimes these efforts are fairly straightforward, but they can also be challenging. With people, the identifiers are usually employee IDs. This is the ideal: numerical identifiers are clean, efficiently stored, and unambiguous. They also protect the privacy of the participants. Proper names are messy identifiers. Not only is there the privacy issue, but there are variants of names—maiden and married, with suffixes attached or not, middle names omitted entirely or truncated to an initial, and so forth. If your participants are something other than people (e.g., branch offices), they will still require an identifier.

Sometimes your data analyst will need to make some sort of transformative magic happen to tie things together. For example, we have seen performance management systems that use an employee ID, a training system that uses proper names, and other systems that use an e-mail address, all within the same organization. We will not get into how common mappings can be created, but a good data analyst will be able to manage this.

The circles in Exhibit 4.1 represent where information about particular participants in the study may reside. Human resource data usually encompasses other types of data, although the overlap may not be perfect.

You may notice that Exhibit 4.1 has areas where data exist only in operations but not in human resources, and so forth. There are often cases where this occurs in practice, although it should not occur in theory. Common explanations for missing data are

- Many personnel data sources have different start and end points and may include records on terminated employees.

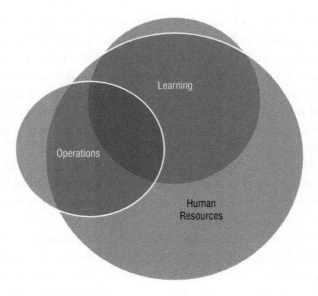

Exhibit 4.1 Participant Data

- ▣ Systems may have different criteria for including and excluding employees, such as terminated employees, summer interns, contract and temporary workers, and more.

- ▣ Some systems may use a convention for identifying employees that does not exist elsewhere (e.g., e-mail addresses are common identifiers in some systems, but not all employees have them).

- ▣ Employees may have slightly different identifiers in different systems. For example, proper names can be problematic in very big employee bases; are "Robert M. Johnson," "Bob Johnson Jr.," and "R. M. Johnson" one person or three? Proper names should be avoided where possible. Loss rates of 5 to 10 percent of the entire data set are not uncommon under these circumstances, although other information, such as birth date or job title, may be used to salvage some of the data.

- ▣ Not all employees belong in all data sets. For example, administrative employees may not be recorded in operational data sets.

- Identifiers may change over time. For example, people may change surnames when married or divorced or may be issued a new employee ID or e-mail address when they change job status.

Human resource data requires you to revisit the important questions about your participants and how they are identified on a regular basis.

DIFFICULTIES IN OBTAINING DATA

"Happy families are all alike; every unhappy family is unhappy in its own way."

—Leo Tolstoy, *Anna Karenina*

As Tolstoy noted about families, unsuccessful data pulls all have their own character, and it is sometimes impossible to anticipate all of the possible difficulties. The Tolstoy quote has been generally appropriated by scientists as shorthand for situations where many conditions need to be true simultaneously, and a single failure creates an overall failure.[11]

Sometimes the problem is not too few systems containing data but too many. In one study we did with Sun Microsystems, the company needed to consolidate five different LMS systems, which existed due to acquisitions and continual development of decentralized learning tools. In these types of situations, the data are not always comparable between different systems, and it is not always possible to consolidate the systems prior to pulling data.

Many difficulties can be described as "politics." For obvious reasons, we will not name names, but here are some of the examples of situations we have witnessed in major corporations:

- We were sent multiple data sets initially, including some sensitive HR files. The senior leader of HR demanded that the information be deleted, which delayed the project for a full year until the proper permissions were obtained. One of our partners on the client side had been a little bit too entrepreneurial in acquiring data for the project and had not obtained the proper approvals prior to sending us the HR data.

■ A highly placed person at a client organization, who was in charge of negotiating the contract, tried to bargain us down in terms of how much data we would receive. The negotiator was in the habit of pushing to give the vendor as little of everything as possible. After explaining very carefully that reducing the amount of data was of advantage to no one, we were able to convince the negotiator to change his strategy. The negotiator was a lawyer, which should surprise no one.

■ Some divisions of a company own certain parts of the business data and share them about as readily as toddlers share toys. Actually, that's not really fair, because toddlers are sometimes in sharing moods and can eventually be taught to behave better.

■ Some stakeholders express apprehension about the results. If they are not very optimistic about what a study will show, they resist getting involved in a project and sharing their data.

■ Some data are stored externally and will require cooperation between different companies. A common situation is that HR data is held by a company that has been used to outsource HR functions. Our experience is that adding the numbers of companies that need to collaborate in this function exponentially increases the difficulty of the task.

Don't despair when difficulties arise in a project. Even in a well-thought-out project plan, perhaps a third of the hypotheses will change once the data collection process begins. Often, the lost hypotheses and missing data can be replaced by new questions and data that were not initially considered.

ETHICS OF MEASUREMENT AND EVALUATION

Many projects require the use of sensitive information, such as career and salary data. It almost goes without saying that this information should be treated as private. We like to consider this a matter of trust, with the same standards of confidentiality that a doctor or a lawyer upholds with clients. There are safeguards that should be taken in any project with this type of sensitive information. First, it is better to use an employee ID than a proper name for several reasons, especially because it makes it harder to reveal the information. You might want to speak to your data analysts about techniques for "hashing" these identifiers in to some form that is unique and reproducible but does not give information to prying eyes. Finally, talk to your IT staff about the computers that the information is kept on and whether it can be transmitted through secure, encrypted channels to safeguard it.

More to the point, during the lifetime of an organization, there are times when hard decisions need to be made. Employee positions, even entire departments, may be eliminated because of performance issues or economic necessity. Some departments may be singled out for special beneficial programs at the expense of others. Certain individuals may receive promotions or other special treatment. The knowledge that you are able to generate using the techniques in this book may provide justification for some of those decisions.

We know how hard it can be to make tough decisions. We wish you wisdom and kindness in your process. As to providing this toolkit to those who make the tough decisions, our conscience is clear, as yours should be if you are using analytics within your own companies: decisions need to be made, regardless of whether the executives in charge have good information or wildly inaccurate information. The choice is obvious: data-driven information is preferable.

When you start a project, it is important to talk to the stakeholders and compliance officers to understand what data are off limits for making decisions. There are cases where having more information to use for a given end can be specifically unethical or illegal. For example, many pharmaceutical companies provide continuing medical education, such as webinars and special lectures, in their area of expertise. It is not only unethical, but actually illegal, to design the information to promote particular products. Financial organizations, such as credit card companies, have rules that govern how personal financial data may be used in marketing. In all industries, race, gender, and age are considered sensitive areas. Whether this information finds its way into the evaluation process or whether the results are released should be part of the considerations for the project. As we said earlier, in a touchy situation, it is usually better to at least know the truth of the matter.

TELLING THE TRUTH

> *Research has demonstrated the impressive human ability to carefully consider evidence and then reach conclusions that are consistent with the conclusion we would like to reach. When people have a stake in reaching a particular conclusion, they tend to focus on evidence that supports the conclusion they would like to reach and evaluate that evidence in an uncritical fashion.*
>
> — Authors K. J. Holyoak and D. Simon[12]

The ethical issues just discussed (protecting privacy, or using information that is unauthorized or inappropriate) enjoy universal agreement, at least in the light of day, and thus do not require much discussion and thought. One problem that often arises in analytics projects is the demand for a particular answer to the evaluation process. We have heard of measurement projects being conducted to "prove" the value of a human capital investment, before the data are even pulled, and where the possibility that the investment has little or no value was not even being considered. We have heard practitioners toss out analysis methods when they failed to confirm their belief in a program, where they clearly would have kept the method and stood behind the accuracy if it provided a convenient, politically acceptable answer. We have seen stakeholders push for assumptions that would increase the ROI based on nothing more than self-interest.

Truly blatant fakery, or the demand for it, is not that common in our experience. The old joke about statistics and bikinis has a lot of truth in it.[13] In our part of the country, college basketball stirs up a lot of passion, and listening to partisan arguments confirms that both parties can be telling the truth, which is to say, lying. Of course, many facts require so many footnotes that it is clear how they were selected. For example, it is common to hear fans claim their team is the best because they win more, while hearing fans from an opposing team make the same claim using different time periods, criteria, and exclusions.[14] This phenomenon has been demonstrated scientifically, not just anecdotally. Princeton and Dartmouth played a particularly rough and contentious game. Researchers had students from each school watch the game film. Students were able to identify twice as many infractions for the opponent as for their own team.[15]

The overarching point is that any reasonably sized project has hundreds of small decisions associated with it, involving looking at some metrics and not others, filtering outliers, deciding on a time frame, gauging what factors are considered in a statistical model, and so on. It sometimes happens, given the combinations of those decisions, that no impact is shown in nineteen out of twenty circumstances, but the twentieth variant is adopted because it shows the right (i.e., desired) answer. We feel strongly that all results should be reported accurately. This responsibility is only heightened by the practical necessity that the intended audience sees only the tip of the vast data iceberg that underlies the conclusions of the project.

First, collaborate with your stakeholders to determine your hypotheses (see Chapter 2 for more information about aligning with stakeholders and creating hypotheses). It is bad scientific practice to reframe hypotheses and make up new mathematical models after the data have been analyzed, because it is easy to pick only the ones that support your prejudices. Parapsychology, the study of extrasensory phenomena, was once much more closely allied to psychology that it is currently. The split occurred largely because parapsychologists would generate data, for example, from card-guessing exercises and look for unusual patterns in the data to analyze, rather than making a prediction up front and seeing whether the data confirmed it, as more serious scientists do. We encourage you to emulate serious scientists, not spook chasers.[16]

Second, one crucial activity to do during stakeholder meetings is to ask the awkward questions, such as, "What actions would be taken if the program turns out to have no effect?" If the question is answered with some potential actions spelled out, your evaluation should be able to proceed in an honest and supportive environmental. If the question generates anger, confusion, or stony silence, there may be serious trouble ahead. We take this activity quite seriously, sometimes asking it in casual social settings of individuals or speaking privately to some members of your team beforehand and asking them to take careful note of facial expressions of crucial stakeholders when the question is dropped.

Third, there are good reasons to analyze data sets thoroughly, but prolonging the analysis for a particular conclusion is not one of them. If your analysis requires a complicated set of filters, exclusions, and changes in the assumptions before the right (i.e., desired) answer appears, it is a sign of trouble.[17] As in the first point, deciding as many of the hypotheses as possible up front and devising the exact tests are an important step in preserving integrity.

U.S. BANK BRANCH MANAGER TRAINING

CASE STUDY

U.S. Bank is the sixth largest commercial bank in the United States. The company provides a comprehensive line of banking, brokerage, insurance, investment, mortgage, trust, and payment services products to consumers, businesses, and institutions.

U.S. Bank's Learning Services is responsible for learning and development for the consumer banking business. Many learning programs are required, with the goal of providing the know-how necessary for the employees to be conversant in their positions at the company. As the U.S. Bank organization continues to grow, leadership and management training is of strategic importance to the company. This study measures the business impact of two learning modules in a training program for U.S. Bank branch managers. The program is known as the Branch Manager Toolbook.

Learning Intervention: Branch Manager Toolbook Modules

The Branch Manager Toolbook is a self-directed learning program designed to help branch managers and assistant branch managers be more effective in their leadership roles at the bank branch level. The Toolbook was created to support the varying levels of skills and experience of the learner. The goal is to efficiently target learning where it is needed, while avoiding duplication where it is not. The program is designed in such a way that the managers can gain access to it online, print it out, and complete various modules at their own pace. The Toolbook is not required learning at the corporate level, but individual regions or districts may recommend or require that their managers go through it. Demonstrating business effectiveness is important in affecting adoption of the learning program.

There are a total of 11 modules in the Toolbook, originally developed in 2002. In 2007, each of these modules was updated. The two modules selected for this analysis contain content related to consumer loans and demand deposits and are based on key organizational performance measures.

Measurement Design

Some of the consumer bank branches with high potentials that were performing below expectations, in one or both of these key performance measures, were the target of this study to see if the revised modules could affect key performance. Large metropolitan markets, including traditional branches and in-store branches, were in the study. Because the participants were not the very lowest performers, it was anticipated that they would gain the most from modest training. The training was taken in September 2007, and the results were tracked over the period of October through December 2007.

Business Impact

The focus of the study was to measure the links between learning outcomes and important strategic factors affecting U.S. Bank's business. The company was interested in knowing whether the two modules of the Manager Toolbook affected branch manager performance, as measured by

1. Demand deposit activity, in terms of (a) more accounts opened, (b) fewer accounts closed, and (c) higher average balances.
2. Consumer loan activity, in terms of (a) more loan applications submitted, (b) more loans booked, and (c) higher dollar value of total loans given.

To determine whether the impact on the business outcomes was attributed to the consumer loan and demand deposit modules of the Toolbook and not any demographic or performance-related variables, statistically significant analyses were conducted by Capital Analytics as follows:

Data were collected on 265 managers who completed the demand deposit module and 251 managers completing the consumer loans module, and a control group of comparable size. In order to determine whether results of

(Continued)

a particular study are statistically significant, it is necessary to have a large-enough sample size and obtain a reasonable amount of variation in the data to have high confidence levels about the measured impact on business outcomes that result from the training intervention. Of critical importance is to be able to state that the outcome measured is related to the intervention and not to other factors that might have influenced the outcomes. The statistical models used in this particular analysis had a confidence level of 98 percent.

Key Findings

Measurement of business impact resulting from training interventions has historically been advanced to justify the expenditure of the training development and deployment in a postintervention analysis, providing little guidance for future action. This U.S. Bank study is a prime example of how measurement of business impact can be used proactively, namely to prioritize and guide future investment decisions.

Here is how the findings relate to this broader decision approach. The analysis definitely demonstrated the favorable impact of the demand deposit training on the level of deposits in the trained group relative to the control group. The ROI from this impact was more than triple digits, far above the corporate investment threshold, providing favorable financial results that more than justified the original training interventions. Of greater significance to bank decision making are the implications for the future.

The detailed organization of the data required to do the analysis provides a roadmap for targeting and further improving the business impact of future training interventions and redesigns—feedback on innovation so often requested by higher management. By stratifying the original data between such key factors as tenure and prior branch performance, the training organization has details useful to make targeted recommendations to upper management.

Analysis results from these segmentations provide the U.S. Bank management team members with the data they need to focus future innovation on the factors with the greatest potential to further enhance business outcomes beyond those documented here. It is this solid analytically defensible foundation for future innovation that is one of the key results of the efforts documented here.

Implications

This study allowed U.S. Bank to determine whether the redesigned curriculum improved the business outcomes produced by branch bank managers taking the training. The analysis gives U.S. Bank the data needed to measure the business impact of future program modifications, as well as broader organizational deployment.

At the branch level, this analysis allowed U.S. Bank senior management to show the impact of the training as it related to specific branch managers' prior performance. The work provides the measurements needed to decide whether mandatory deployment across the entire organization has potential business value. Furthermore, the analysis provides the framework to experiment in the benefits of alternate delivery modalities, such as traditional classroom and e-learning platforms, for more interactive learning.

SUMMARY

For a successful measurement initiative, you will want to draw data from at least two or three major sources around the organization. The most influential data will likely be operational data. Data from human resource information systems (HRIS) play an important part of most projects. Also, learning management systems (LMS) contain information about training, which is a common focus of human capital investment measurements. Social media and informal learning systems are becoming more and more important. Engagement surveys are effective instruments for gauging sentiment by employees. Sometimes interviewing is a good way to understand a business process before a more rigorous analysis can be undertaken. Data generated entirely outside the organization, such as benchmarking, may play a role in measurement.

Knowing the data's location isn't sufficient. Your data retrieval effort will doubtless require some careful thought and problem solving along the way. Organizational politics is a rich source of challenges you may have to solve. A key goal is to have the correct "keys" or records that will let you tie different data sets together. Remember that you are working with a precious resource within the organization, and care is required as you take on this responsibility. It is important to realize that these data represent the work of the company's most precious resource, and you need to be aware of people's privacy and the responsibility that you are taking on by creating the knowledge required for major human resource decisions. Part of that trust is to provide accurate results and try to stay above the pressures that will be placed on you for predetermined conclusions.

NOTES

1. T. Hastie, R. Tibshirani, and J. Friedman, *The Elements of Statistical Learning: Data Mining, Inference, and Prediction,* 2nd ed. (New York: Spring Science+ Business Media, 2009). These authors, colleagues of Deming, note the quote is widely attributed to him, although there seems to be no concrete verification.

2. E. W. Pugh, *Memories That Shaped an Industry: Decisions Leading to IBM System/360* (Boston: MIT Press, 1984).

3. B. Byerly and J. Campbell, "Measuring the Impact of Social Media and Information Sharing," *Invited Webinar,* February 25, 2010, American Society of Training and Development; B. Byerly, *YouTube meets iTunes: Evaluating the Impact of Social Media Projects* (Orlando: Society for Applied Learning Technology, 2010).

4. E. Krell, "Personality Counts," *HR Magazine* vol. 50, no. 11 (2005).

5. C. Youssef and F. Luthans "Human, Social, and Now Positive Psychological Capital Management: Investing in People for Competitive Advantage," *Organizational Dynamics* vol. 33, no. 2 (2004): 143–160.

6. E. Loftus and J. C. Palmer, "Reconstruction of Automobile Destruction: An Example of the Interaction between Language and Memory," *Journal of Verbal Learning and Verbal Behavior* vol. 13 (1974): 585–589.

7. S. D. Dubner, *Freakonomics: A Rogue Economist Explores the Hidden Side of Everything* (New York: William Morrow, 2005).

8. K. Barnett and J. Berk, *Human Capital Analytics: Measuring and Improving Learning and Talent Impact* (Tarentum, PA: Word Association, 2007); P. P. Phillips and J. J. Phillips, *ROI In Action Casebook (Measurement and Evaluation)* (San Francisco: Pfeiffer, 2008).

9. J. Diamond, *Guns, Germs, and Steel: The Fates of Human Societies* (New York: W. W. Norton and Company, 2007).

10. S. Adams, "Dilbert," Dilbert.com, United Feature Syndicate, April 30, 2008.

11. Diamond, *Guns, Germs, and Steel.*

12. K. J. Holyoak and D. Simon "Bidirectional Reasoning in Decision Making by Constraint Satisfaction," *Journal of Experimental Psychology: General* vol. 128 (1999): 3–31.

13. "What they reveal is very interesting, what they conceal may be vital." We are also fond of Twain's quip that there were three kinds of lies: "Lies, damnable lies, and statistics."

14. For those unfamiliar with college basketball, the correct answer can be taken as "Duke," without further debate.

15. Hastdorf and Cantril, "They Saw the Game: A Case Study," *Journal of Abnormal and Social Psychology* vol. 49, no. 1 (1954): 129–134.

16. J. B. Rhine, *Extra-Sensory Perception* (Boston: Bruce Humphries, 1934).

17. A slang expression that describes this process is "waterboarding the data," indicating that the data, if placed under sufficient duress, will "confess" to anything, whether it did it or not.

CHAPTER 5

What Dashboards Are Telling You: Descriptive Statistics and Correlations

"Most often when we see illogical behavior, the fault is in the measurement system, not in the employees!"

—Brian Joiner[1]

Today, most HR organizations have some method of reporting data on their activities. These methods can be as simple as an Excel spreadsheet kept on a user's desktop or may involve specialized or custom-written tools involving databases or business intelligence. The reports that come out of these data sources can be called descriptive statistics. The reports might be a few tables or graphs from a spreadsheet, dashboard-like reporting mechanisms, or other specialized tools such as SAS Enterprise BI Server. The goal of a descriptive statistic is to provide a quick indicator of what is going on in the organization, such as: What is the headcount? Who completed what training? How much is payroll? The information from these sources would generally be presented in some kind of dashboard and/or scorecard. The word *correlation* can be used in various ways. In our case, correlation is when various key performance indicators tend to vary according to the circumstances. For example, if we see that sales are higher in the Eastern region, we say that the sales are correlated with region.

DESCRIPTIVE STATISTICS

This book has hinted at preferences for "heavy statistics" of the sort that require some sort of specialized mathematical knowledge to fully implement. So, why talk about the simpler things? There are many good reasons. First, basic descriptive statistics are a good check on what is happening with your business processes. Any time you walk into a doctor's office, whether it's a university teaching hospital or a bush clinic in a tent, someone takes your pulse and temperature. This sort of basic triage is fundamental to understanding your data. Measuring basic values provides several major benefits. In the early stages of a major data collection process, descriptive statistics allow you to present interim findings to your stakeholders. This keeps everyone informed and has the potential to catch fundamental errors. In a quickly changing data landscape, descriptive statistics keep people informed when there isn't time for a lengthier analysis. Descriptive statistics also aid analysts in becoming familiar with the data sets in a way that helps them detect patterns and begin asking tougher questions of the data. Once the more complex analysis is done, we recommend that you do not communicate findings in the language of esoteric mathematics but, rather, in short and simple terms, with garden-variety graphics. Early descriptive statistics lay the groundwork.

Descriptive statistics is the first stage of the measurement journey. They ensure that everyone is speaking the same language from the very beginning. Descriptive statistics in dashboards allow quick and simple real-time updates where business processes require fast-moving attention. Finally, there are often cases in projects where companies have developed such preconceived myths around their data that even the most basic assumptions go unchallenged. We have seen cases where "mandatory" training programs reached only 40 percent of the population, where assumptions about which region of the country had the highest sales were years out of date, and ideas about "average" profit margin were off by more than 50 percent. Descriptive statistics, not arcane math that would puzzle a physics professor, were the mechanism by which these myths were debunked.

Descriptive statistics are quantitative descriptions of the main features of a collection of data.[2] We define them as basic numerical indicators, one number taken at a time, that do not require advanced mathematics or explanations: averages, maximum and minimum values, and some breakdowns by categories. Informally, you might think of descriptive statistics as the level of analysis a sportscaster might use to communicate with an audience. For example, the shooting percentage in basketball is a descriptive statistic that summarizes the performance of a player or a team.

In most cases, descriptive statistics summarize data from a single source (we will expand our discussion of descriptive statistics later in this chapter). They provide simple ways to look at activities and can be presented in simple-to-read graphs and charts.

Dashboards provide an at-a-glance view of key performance indicators (KPIs) relevant to a particular objective or business process (e.g., sales, marketing, human resources, or production). The term *dashboard* originates from the automobile dashboard where drivers monitor the major functions at a glance. Dashboards represent a snapshot of the business that can alert you to realize (or recognize) that something is wrong or everything is running smoothly. For years, people in the corporate world have tried to come up with a solution that would tell them whether their business needed maintenance or if the temperature of their business was running above normal. Dashboards typically are limited to showing summaries, key trends, comparisons, and exceptions.[3]

GOING GRAPHIC WITH THE DATA

Effective representation of the data is the first step to making it understandable. Many people in the corporate world believe that graphics are essential to a good-looking, credible report. Similarly, friends in elementary school were certain that putting a report in a binder was good for an extra letter grade. We are not aware of any research on the topic but suspect there was truth to it. Therefore, providing ample graphs and charts is a standard part of our methodology.

In all seriousness, our experience has shown us that the eye is a good statistician. What we mean by that is that a good representation of the data allows the layman to have insights similar to those achieved by difficult math. Many insights have emerged from visual representations of the data that were previously missed when the information was presented only in tables.

When well done, graphics are an invaluable tool for exploring your data space. However, they must go beyond just looking good and must offer true insights into your research.

DATA OVER TIME

Graphing the value of data over time, or *trend line analysis*, can be invaluable for informing you of possible future states. For example, are employee engagement scores going up? Is absenteeism improving or getting worse? Is employee turnover in a critical position increasing? Exhibit 5.1 has a trend line added, which is a line best fitted to the data.

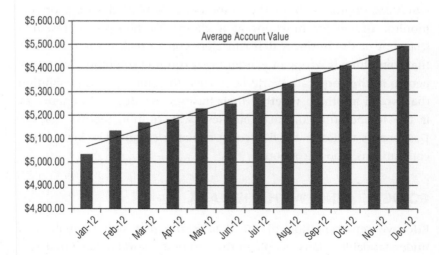

Exhibit 5.1 Bar Graph over Time

Remember, however, that all you need to make a line is two points, and it may not illustrate what is really going on. In Exhibit 5.1, it is possible that performance peaks in December and goes into a steady decline thereafter.

Be very discerning when you make forecasts using simple historical data. Using trend-line analysis to make decisions about the future may be risky due to shallow levels of analysis that are no longer correlated to actual drivers. The status quo has a way of being disrupted. Furthermore, who says things continue in a straight line? Some types of data may increase in a straight line; other types may level out, peak and decline, show seasonal cycles, or just be a gigantic mess that never settles out to any sensible pattern at all. Exhibit 5.2 shows closing ratios for a technology company during a two-year period. If the graph is laid out with year 2 superimposed on top of year 1, as shown in Exhibit 5.2, there are clearly some effects of seasonality, with peaks in June and December. We first encountered this particular data set during a client project. We were considering measuring a program based on the prior year data that was available up through October, but because so many deals close late in the year, we delayed the project until the end-year data were available.

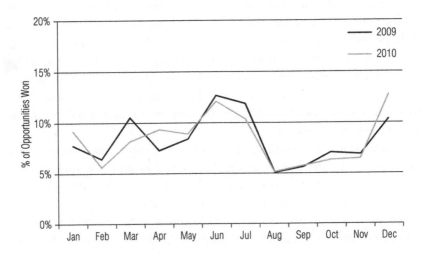

Exhibit 5.2 Line Graph over Time

DESCRIPTIVE STATISTICS ON STEROIDS

Returning to our sports analogy, sometimes it is useful to combine data from multiple sources. For example, information about an athlete's high school, previous season, or how the person compares to other athletes from his or her state may improve our understanding of the athlete's current performance.

Combining the information from the two dashboards and then adding finance and operational data (such as sales or production data, depending on the human capital investment) will give you a more robust and deeper understanding of your workforce. Our phrase *descriptive statistics on steroids* is the result of combining information from data sets that are not usually brought together for analysis in an organization.

The intersection of this data may offer insights, for example, into what type of employees (tenure, gender, education, and so on) have completed which training curriculum and are outperforming their peers. It may give you insights into diversity issues that you would not be able to see using a one-dimensional dashboard.

One of our clients, Chrysler, featured in a case study for this chapter. Chrysler looked at data from three systems: LMS, HRIS, and the CRM (customer relationship management). The combined data clearly showed that a fully trained salesperson sold significantly more units than an untrained one, that location size played a role in a salesperson's performance, and that tenure was also influencing his or her performance. These insights suggested possible correlations with demographics and other factors that were influencing performance. Without viewing the combined descriptive statistics from three systems, these insights into patterns of performance would have remained buried.

Data from three different sources, retention, absenteeism, and training rates, are shown in Exhibits 5.3, 5.4, and 5.5. Individually, they are somewhat informative. However, the real insights emerge from Exhibit 5.6, which shows an overlay of the retention and training rates in a line graph. This graph suggests that training rates and retention rates rise and fall together, a hypothesis that is likely worth

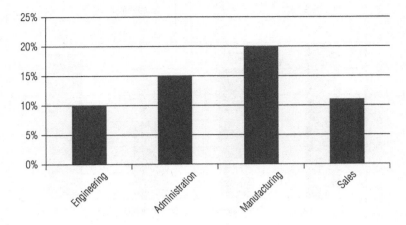

Exhibit 5.3 Turnover Rate

investigating further. This is not the product of any sophisticated analysis, only a few minutes of fiddling with the data in a spreadsheet. This example of "stats on steroids"—the power gained in an analysis by combining information from different business intelligence sources within the organization—supports our argument that basic descriptive data is a great starting point for any analysis.

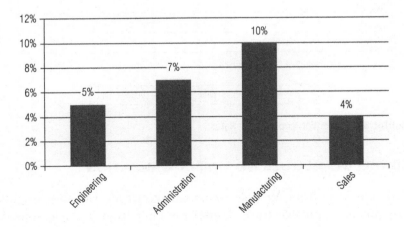

Exhibit 5.4 Absenteeism

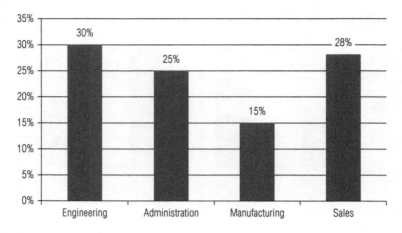

Exhibit 5.5 Training Rate

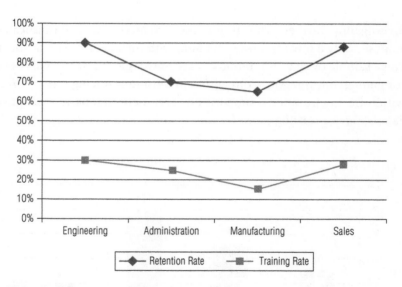

Exhibit 5.6 Retention and Training Rates

CORRELATION DOES NOT IMPLY CAUSATION

Gathering data from multiple sources may provide valuable insights that are not available from dashboards built from a single source. However, we advise caution when making decisions solely based on these data. In many cases, the data presented on dashboards are correlated (i.e., metrics are related and moving in the same or opposite directions), but that does not always imply causality—that one event has an influence on the other. The conventional dictum that "correlation does not imply causation" means that correlation cannot be used to infer a causal relationship between the variables.[4]

Whenever we discover a correlation between two outcomes, we look to see whether there might some other factors or behaviors that are correlated to the same outcome. For example, it is commonly known that there is a high statistical correlation between ice cream sales and deaths due to drowning. Does that mean that we should abolish all ice cream sales to lower drowning? Of course not. When it is warm, more people go swimming. Hence more people drown. When it is warm, more people eat ice cream. Is the weather the cause? Or a coincidence? Perhaps drowning is caused by something else, such as carelessness or an inability to swim.

Other examples of highly correlated variables:

- The weight of elementary schoolchildren and their math scores on a standardized test.
- The number of firefighters called to a fire and the amount of damage caused by the fire.
- The height of an elementary school student and his or her reading level.
- The stock market is alleged to be tied to all sorts of amusing indicators, from sales of aspirin, lipstick, men's underwear, women's skirt length, who won the Super Bowl or the White House, the amount of snow in Boston, and the average attractiveness of waiters and waitresses.
- Childhood obesity rates and safety warnings on playground equipment.
- Consumption of milk and death rates.

Recalling the Chrysler study mentioned earlier, its executives knew that training and sales metrics were correlated. In fact, as we stated, they knew that trained sales consultants outsold their untrained counterparts by a significant amount per year. Yet no one had been able to establish a causal link proving that training was the factor responsible for such a big difference (as opposed to other factors driving individual and business performance). The training department, therefore, had little influence with its peers in other business units.

The intense interest in these correlated sales metrics helped identify areas for further exploration. As a result, Capital Analytics was engaged to conduct a business impact study. The training department was unable to make decisions or show proof of impact based on correlations alone, but it could begin to dig into what was happening in the field and determine the role of training in driving sales representatives' performance. Using an advanced statistical modeling technique, the true relationship was revealed: although better salespeople were the ones selected for training, much of the improvement could be attributed to training.

CASE STUDY

CHRYSLER ACADEMY, DEALERSHIP SALES CONSULTANT TRAINING, PART 1

Chrysler Academy is responsible for designing and delivering sales training to the sales consultants in the network of more than 3,000 dealerships. Training and sales numbers were correlated metrics at Chrysler. In fact, Chrysler knew that trained sales consultants outsold their untrained counterparts by 35 vehicles per year, but no one had been able to establish a causal link proving that training was the factor responsible for those 35 vehicles (as opposed to other factors driving individual and business performance). The Chrysler Academy, therefore, had little ground on which to stand when compared to its peers in other business units. Marketing touted exciting ads, and the credit group boasted of attractive financing packages for driving vehicle sales (see Exhibit 5.7).

In addition to Chrysler Academy's internal reputation being at stake, there were also challenges with the dealers. Chrysler's dealers are the academy's customers and pay to send their sales consultants to training. Due to the high turnover of new sales consultants, dealers were reluctant to send their consultants to training until they had proved they would stick around. The academy postulated that lack of training was correlated with high turnover, but once again, it had no conclusive proof to leverage with the dealers.

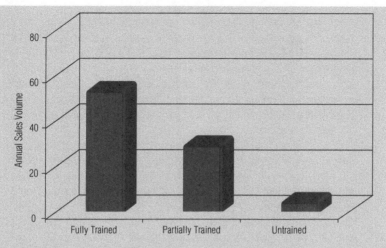

Exhibit 5.7 Correlation: Training's Impact on Sales
Reprinted with permission from Chrysler Academy

These correlated metrics, both hot-button issues for Chrysler Academy, helped identify areas for further exploration. The academy couldn't make decisions or show proof of impact based on correlations alone, but it could begin to dig into what was happening in the field and determine the role that training played in driving sales consultants' performance and turnover.

See Chapter 6 for the continuation of this case study.

VF CORPORATION — MAXIMIZING PERFORMANCE

CASE STUDY

Background

VF Corporation is a global apparel company that owns such brands as the North Face, Wrangler, Vans, Lee, 7 for All Mankind, Nautica, JanSport, and many others. Although many of these brands are VF's legacy brands, the company has grown largely through acquisition in recent years. Today's portfolio represents diverse markets and cultures. VF's leaders recognized the need to unify the brands and drive a high-performance culture across the disparate divisions, locations, and brands.

(Continued)

In 2010, VF launched Maximizing Performance, a company-wide performance management process, to support their goal of building a culture of achievement and to improve business results. A key component in VF's development of a high-performance culture was getting all associates aligned with corporate goals. With unique cultures across their many brands, VF wanted the associates to understand how their individual job roles and departments contributed to their brand and how their brand contributed to the company as a whole.

VF determined that a key indicator of progress toward a high-performance culture was the annual engagement survey. VF believed that the activities and behaviors encouraged by Maximizing Performance would be linked to improved individual performance and engagement, and that these would be linked to profitability. VF partnered with Capital Analytics to explore the connections between employee participation in Maximizing Performance, employee performance, and engagement during the rollout of Maximizing Performance. One goal of the study was to help VF understand, during deployment, how to make adjustments to continually improve the new process.

The Study

VF's stakeholders selected two brands to include in this business impact study: Brand A is a recently acquired, young, trendy brand, while brand B is a legacy brand with a long and rich history. Each represents a different workforce and culture, with younger vs. older workforces and contemporary vs. traditional products. VF's stakeholders agreed that these brands were different enough from each other to provide a representative view of participation, engagement, and ultimately the business impact of the new performance management process across the full portfolio of brands. The study focused on U.S.-based, salaried associates of brand A and brand B and considered Maximizing Performance activities from January 2010 through June 2011. The evaluation was designed in three phases, mirroring VF's rollout process for Maximizing Performance (see Exhibit 5.8).

Phase One

Phase one focused on the development of performance plans, analyzing compliance (presence of a plan), and the quality of the plans themselves.

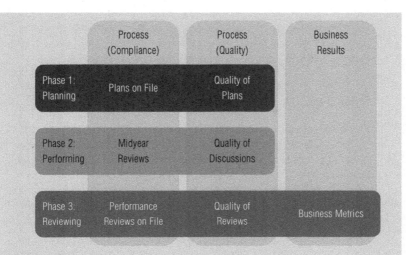

Exhibit 5.8 3 Phases of Maximizing Performance Measurement
Reprinted with permission from VF

The performance plans included objectives, competencies, and individual development plans. The stakeholders hypothesized that having a plan, and especially a high-quality performance plan, would be an indicator of employee commitment, showing that they understand how they connect and contribute to the organization. The researchers evaluated the quality of plans using a weighted rubric. Having a plan, and especially a good-quality plan, would be the first step toward building a high-performance culture.

In phase one, it became clear that a particular population was not engaged in Maximizing Performance: administrative contributors. Appreciating that a high-performance culture needs to be inclusive of all employees, this finding led VF to explore underlying causes. VF discovered that managers simply did not know how to create good goals and development plans for their administrative contributors. In response, VF increased efforts to support managers in engaging administrative contributors in the process.

Early in the Maximizing Performance process, associates expressed confusion over the difference between job descriptions, goals, objectives, and development plans. The evaluation of plan quality quantified this confusion. Because clear and measurable goals are key to Maximizing Performance, VF recognized the need for further training and communication to clarify these important concepts. As evidence of the value of having clear and measurable goals, managers of employees who had good plans (and the

(Continued)

employees themselves) acknowledged that feedback and reviews were easier, less confrontational, and more productive, due to these clearly spelled-out goals.

Phase Two

Phase two consisted of tracking ongoing progress against performance plans and providing developmental feedback to improve performance. From the outset, the manager's explicit role in Maximizing Performance was to assist with plan development and revisions and to provide interim reviews, coaching, and feedback. It was hypothesized that regular discussions around performance would improve goal attainment, as well as engagement. A custom survey captured associate and manager perceptions of this process (see Exhibit 5.9).

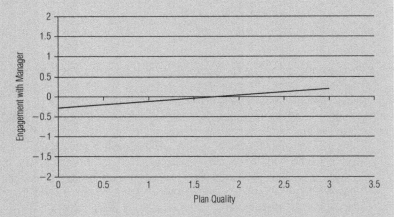

Exhibit 5.9 Engagement with Manager and Plan Quality
Reprinted with permission from VF

Overall, with both brands, the prominent driver of compliance, quality of plans, and engagement was the presence of a manager who participated fully in Maximizing Performance. In light of this finding, VF focused on manager participation, believing that the act of a manager supporting an associate in the development of his or her plan would help associates feel more con-nected to the business and result in improved individual performance and increased engagement scores. The data supported this belief. Both brands showed a high associate compliance rate of more than 90 percent when the manager had a performance plan on file. Furthermore, manager involvement was also linked to higher-quality performance plans. Notably, associates with high-quality plans reported increased levels of engagement with their manager.

Phase Three

Phase three focused on the annual performance appraisal process. Here stakeholders hypothesized that associates with higher-quality plans (better aligned with the business) would earn better performance reviews and would report higher levels of engagement. Performance reviews, turnover data, promotion and salary records, and the annual engagement survey provided data for the analysis.

Phase three did not reveal links between Maximizing Performance and the business metrics evaluated. VF has speculated that the leading indicators of success are present (those seen in phases one and two), and it will take more time for impact to appear in the other metrics. A follow-up study that allows additional time for impact to be manifested may reveal deeper insights into performance reviews, turnover data, promotion and salary records, and the annual engagement survey.

Conclusion

VF continues to deploy Maximizing Performance with the knowledge that engaged managers are essential to the development of a high-performance culture. Engaged managers encourage their associates to participate in their own professional development process. Explicitly showing employees how they contribute to the company's goals is improving engagement at VF and fostering a high-performance culture.

SUMMARY

Descriptive statistics found generally in dashboards and scorecards are the foundation of your analytics efforts. Combining data sets from different systems together produces intelligence synergies. You can discover things in the organization that might have previously gone unnoticed. A very small amount of math and graphical representation will go a long, long way in helping you understand your business structure and processes, but be careful about making decisions on future investments based solely on correlations!

NOTES

1. B. Joiner, *Fourth Generation Management: The New Business Consciousness* (New York: McGraw-Hill, 1994), 242.

2. S. Maxwell and H. Delaney, *Designing Experiments and Analyzing Data: A Model Comparison Perspective* (Belmont, CA: Wadsworth Publishing, 1989).

3. V. Hetherington, *The Dashboard Demystified: What Is a Dashboard?* September 23, 2009, retrieved May 8, 2012, from Dashboard Insight, www.dash boardinsight.com/articles/digital-dashboards/fundamentals/the-dashboard-demystified.aspx.

4. J. Aldrich, "Correlations Genuine and Spurious in Pearson and Yule," *Statistical Science* 10, no. 4 (1995): 364–376.

CHAPTER 6

Causation: What Really Drives Performance

"Shallow men believe in luck or in circumstance. . . .
Strong men believe in cause and effect."

—Ralph Waldo Emerson[1]

Curiously, there is a clear-cut correlation between ice cream consumption and murder rates. Yet is it fair to say that one causes the other? When more data are considered, both ice cream and murder also correlate with drowning, shark attacks, and boating accidents. Does ice cream indeed cause murderous behavior? And is it consumed by sharks? Hardly . . . Unpleasantly hot weather often causes people to be frustrated and irritable. Plus, more people are congregating together outdoors. Thus, conflicts leading to murders become more likely. Hot weather, in rather obvious ways, leads people to indulge in ice cream and water sports to cool off. In turn, water sports leads to more boating accidents and shark attacks. For those who are fond of ice cream, it is equally accurate and fair to say that ice cream prevents snow avalanches and reduces colds and flu. These links are all correlations and thus do not say much about actual causes.

What is a proof of causation, really? How can we establish the connection between an investment and a business effect or say which metric drives another? What we would like to know is which investments change our business for the better. Experimenters and philosophers debate endlessly over what constitutes "proof." Our intuition about what someone will take as "proof" is a bit like game theory—a proof stands until someone creates a counterargument or an alternative explanation, and then the ball is in the other court. We recognize that it is difficult to fully prove something, but we want a good compromise between logical, sound decision making and what is feasible in an enterprise.

Authors Wayne Cascio and John Boudreau articulate a nice set of criteria for causation:[2]

> In fact, there are three necessary conditions to support the conclusion that x causes y. The first is that y did not occur until after x. The second requirement is that x and y can be shown to be related. The third (and most difficult) requirement is that other explanations of the relationship between x and y can be eliminated as plausible rival hypotheses.

The logic in their statement is clear and easily understood. The elegant "3 factors" approach described by Boudreau ends with quite a caveat—"if all other factors can be ruled out"—which is far easier said than done. We will not give a rigorous set of criteria, because our own project work ranges from conclusions we would be comfortable presenting in a scientific journal down to "better information than we had before." Of course, we always aim for the strongest possible proof of causation, but we are realists. Our approach is always a blend of statistics and the best-articulated case the chain of evidence provides. We look for anecdotal evidence, success stories, and any other supporting evidence that tells the same story as the math and logic.

Of course, there are many, many factors that people attempt to use (and even more that they demand from their competitors). One technique experimenters like is randomization. Randomization is using some sort of random mechanism, such as drawing cards or rolling dice, to determine who is in the test group and the control group. Most experiments like subjects to be "blind," which is where the purpose of the experiment is not explained to them until afterward. Another, even more rigorous condition is "double blind," where data is interpreted by people who do not know whether it came from the test or the control group. For example, in an experimental drug trial, the people collecting the data (such as measuring blood pressure) are not told whether the person being measured received the drug or a placebo. Social scientists Thomas Cook and Donald Campbell cite 14 separate threats to validity. These are examples of how far researchers are willing to go in the pursuit of accurate conclusions. Clearly, most are not going to apply in an HR setting. We have read only a few articles in the business literature where randomization of subjects occurred.[3] It is rare when HR personnel have this kind of latitude. Concepts such as placebos or double-blind rating are clearly silly to even discuss in an HR or learning and development (L&D) context.

Ultimately, proof is a combination of mathematics and old-fashioned reasoning and argumentation. It is always possible that factors outside a study—the economy, the weather—may have affected things in ways that were unanticipated. Scientific fields are revolutionized by discoveries that lay waste to careful work done with the best intentions. The newspapers document the release of erroneously convicted people. However, we cannot give up on the pursuit of science, justice, or an accurate measurement of human capital analytics. We do the best we can and try to bring more certainty to the field than existed previously.

Scientific reasoning has been around, to some extent or the other, since ancient Greece. HR and L&D departments have not been as rigorously applying these concepts as, say, theoretical physicists. However, there are many areas where analysis techniques are applied, such as by actuaries, in the accounting department, in marketing deployment, in supply chain optimization, and so forth. Our background was eclectic. That allowed us to bring in techniques from psychology, statistics, economics, education, and computer science and marry them with business common sense. The most important aspects we look at in our work are described in the following sections.

CAN YOU CREATE SEPARATE TEST AND CONTROL GROUPS?

One of the first things we look for is the ability to separate out test and control groups. Where Boudreau's criteria for causation was separated based on time, the fact that x occurred before y was a necessary condition. We think more in terms of some group receiving x, and some other group not getting x, and looking for the differences between them. Test and control groups have been around a long time; the concept of sugar pills being used to assess the impact of actual medications has been around since the nineteenth century.[4] Sugar pills have an important difference from training, however, in that they allow an experiment to be blind—the subjects in a drug trial have no way of knowing whether they have received the medication or a harmless substitute. It is difficult to contrive a situation in most human capital investments where the subjects of the study do not know they have received the intervention. An interesting analogy exists between drug trials and training, however. There is a well-established placebo effect that shows an improvement in subjects who believe they have been given something efficacious. In industrial psychology, we speak of the Hawthorne effect, which postulates that productivity increases in workplace settings when something is being measured.[5]

There is a key difference between establishing test and control groups in a clinical drug trial and doing so to isolate the impact of a human capital investment: the groups in the drug trial are contrived for the purposes of testing the drug, while the test and control groups for a human capital measurement study tend to be naturally occurring because of the way the investment is deployed. In virtually every case we have come across, there were significant differences in the performance of the test and control groups.

There may not be a bright line between a test and a control group. The majority of human capital investments are rolled out over time, and even if an investment is applied to an entire company, it is unusual for everyone in the company to receive the investment at the same time. This allows people who have not *yet* received the investment to be treated as the control group. Some people may not receive the investment in its entirety, and some people may be missed entirely.

We have done a number of studies where a program that was sup-posedly applied to "everyone" actually missed hundreds of people. This was discovered only during the "descriptive statistics" phase of the study.

As before, if you think outside the box when it comes to defining participants, you may be able to find test and control groups that naturally occur. For example, we have done studies where the parti-cipants were not individuals but branch offices. The test group was a branch office where everyone was trained, and the control group was an office where no one was trained. There are a number of possible variations on this theme: less than half trained and more than half trained, none trained, some trained, all trained, and so forth.

ARE THERE OBSERVABLE DIFFERENCES?

Was there a measurable positive effect? Did things get better for the trainees (or, in some cases, not decline when the control group did or decline less)? Was an improvement seen? Was the change statistically significant, or could it be a product of random chance? Statistics pro-vides objective criteria. If there were 50 people in both the test and the control groups, and all 50 in the test group improved, while none did in the control group, the conclusion is clear. Usually, however, there is a mix: perhaps 30 in the test group improved, and only 20 in the control group did. Statistics provides methods for assigning a likelihood that a particular outcome was the result of an underlying pattern, rather than just through random variation.

DID YOU CONSIDER PRIOR PERFORMANCE?

A crucial component to establishing causation is examining prior performance. In almost no cases do those selected for training or some other intervention look the same as those who did not get the investment. Sometimes people are put into a training program as a reward; sometimes it is the last step to rehabilitate an inferior employee, short of termination. Self-selection is usually one of the strongest biases, mostly in a positive direction. Any time there is data about the employee's performance prior to the beginning of a program, it is important to collect that data and determine how the test and control groups differ. One of the best types of variables (predictors) to use is a difference variable, such as, "What was the change after the training program?" Of course, that question makes the most sense for the test group; you will need to figure out a comparable period of time for the control group.

An example of selection bias is what we refer to as "the milk story." Among the United States' problems in the Great Depression of the 1930s were hungry schoolchildren and a surplus of unsold dairy products. Some thoughtful and well-intentioned person decided to have the government buy up the surplus milk and give it to school-children, thus killing two birds with one stone. Another well-intentioned person decided to measure the effect of the program and asked schoolteachers to randomly select half of the class and give them milk, and measure the children later. Lo and behold, the measurement effort showed that milk made you shorter, sicker, and weaker. The explanation generally accorded at this point was that teachers had, consciously or unconsciously, selected the neediest children for the milk supplements. The moral of the story is that where people end up depends, at least to some extent, on where they started. Or maybe the moral is that milk is bad for you. We forget sometimes.

DID YOU CONSIDER TIME-RELATED CHANGES?

Have you accounted for the effects of time? Changes over time can be particularly difficult to explain, especially in cases where the study looks at changes like advertising or a benefits program that affects everyone in the entire company equally. In these types of cases, the general plan is to notice whether metrics improved and take credit for it, or if metrics declined, try to avoid blame. This is of course not the scientific method we prefer. Time effects may be impossible to entirely figure out. But a good start is to look rigorously at changes over time. Time changes may be general upward or downward trends and may have aspects of seasonality (e.g., some industries experience a slowdown in the summer). This is the reason we encourage graphing performance over time for the descriptive statistics aspect of the project.

DID YOU LOOK AT THE DESCRIPTIVE STATISTICS?

Have you understood all possible relevant demographic implications? When prior performance is available, this is less of a problem, because the baseline performance allows an apples-to-apples comparison. The relationship between the metrics and the demographics should be considered as thoroughly as possible. This gets back to the "selection bias" problem, because there are big demographic differences in the test and control groups.

HAVE YOU CONSIDERED THE RELATIONSHIP BETWEEN THE METRICS?

What are the relationships between the metrics? When multiple metrics are available, it is necessary to consider the interrelationship between the different values—are there correlations, and are they positive or negative? Are unit sales stronger, but at the expense of profitability? In one example, we saw a call center where training improved sales rates. However, the strongest driver of sales was time spent per call, so the actual mechanism was that training caused the agents to spend more time per call, and the extra time increased sales. The really interesting part was that the amount of money expended on the extra time per call was not covered by the marginal extra values of the sales. The training did the job that it was asked to do, but unfortunately, the net effect on the business was a loss.

These factors—test and control, prior performance, and a complete analysis of demographics and time—taken together, are what we consider before discussing impact on a study. Remember, "softer" data, such as interviews, success stories, and reaction to the investment, will be important to telling a good story and should be consistent with the quantitative data.

A GENTLE INTRODUCTION TO STATISTICS

During the last few decades, a wide range of tools and techniques have emerged to analyze data. Given the opportunities this presents, we want to give you a sense of what is possible. There are two concepts that loom fairly large in what we do. The first is the idea of certainty. The second is the idea of impact.

Certainty is the sense you get of how likely something did not occur by chance. Suppose a friend comes up to you one day, flips a coin, and it lands heads up. He tells you it's a magic coin, much more likely to land on heads than tails, and offers to sell you the coin. You are extremely skeptical. After all, it might be a perfectly normal coin; he may have just changed his story slightly had the coin landed on tails. Suppose he flips the coin again, and it lands on heads again. You are still unimpressed; after all, if you flipped a coin twice, one time in four it might end up with two heads. But what if he flips it three times, and they are all heads? Four? You might begin to pay attention. Would 19 heads out of 20 make you take notice? What about 40 out of 50? At some point, you will increasingly acknowledge that this coin may in fact be something out of the ordinary. But what *is* that point?

This is exactly the sort of question we struggle with every day, although the questions are much more complicated. What if 15 out of 20 trainees improved their performance, and only 11 out of 20 in the control group did so? How much more certain could we be if those numbers were doubled? Statistics has various methods for answering these sorts of questions with precise numbers.

A couple of different kinds of factors can go into these tests of statistical significance. The results are statistical models. Most of our models can be expressed like this:

Outcome variable = Function of (one or more input variables)

Thus, the above example might be expressed as:

Number of improved performances
    = Function of (whether they received the investment or not)

In other words, does whether the person received the investment help us predict whether he or she will do better? Of course, any number of factors might go into our assessment of whether the person might be expected to improve. Perhaps we are talking about sales performance, and we know that those with higher salary bases are

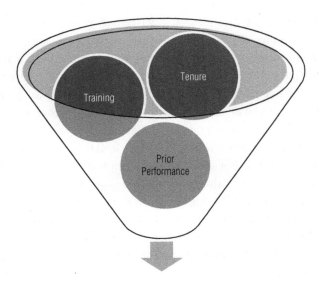

Exhibit 6.1 Sample Function—One Metric

maxed out in their performance, so we should account for that factor. Perhaps there are four regions of the country that we have data from, and we need to take that into account. Note that there is always a single outcome variable, or key performance indicator, on the left side of the equals sign, and there may be any number of factors on the right. Notice that some of these factors might fall into categories (such as training status or gender), and some are continuous numbers that might vary over a range (such as salary or tenure within the organization).

Exhibit 6.1 shows an example of what a function is. Several items can go in, but only one number comes out.

BASIC IDEAS BEHIND REGRESSION

Regression modeling is a popular technique that can be used to quantify the relationship between two or more variables. When applied to human capital, it can look at historical data that measure an HR action, intervention, or investment and determine whether outcomes measured at a later point in time are the result of those earlier actions, interventions, or investments. For example, let's say a company decides to spend money on training for customer service employees. To determine whether the investment was worthwhile, it compares the sales for a six-month period before and after the training. If it sees an increase in sales (while controlling for other changes), it might determine that for every dollar spent on training, there is an increase of $1.50 in sales. Then a simplified depiction of the regression model would be: Sales = 1.50 × Training dollars.

There are many other methodologies similar to regression that are even more powerful. For example, you might want to factor in categorical variables such as the geographic region or the season; general linear models allow combining categorical and continuous variables in the same model. Structural equation modeling is much like regression, but it allows models where the variables have complex interdependencies or hierarchies. In human capital analytics, the analysis can become very complex.

MODEL FIT AND STATISTICAL SIGNIFICANCE

When evaluating a model, we look for the overall fit of the model, as well as its statistical significance. Depending on the type of model, there are statistical measures that tell us how well the model explains the relationship we are measuring. One simple measure is R^2 (R-squared). It tells us what percentage of the variation in the data is explained by the model. So in our regression model measuring the relationship between customer service training and increased sales, we find that our R^2 is 60 percent. This means that 60 percent of the increase in sales can be directly linked to the increase in our training investment.

Another aspect of our analysis is our certainty with the results. This is determined by the level of statistical significance or confidence. The main drivers are the quantity and variability of the data. In business, 95 percent is a fairly standard and acceptable level of confidence. So, for our example, this means that there is a 5 percent chance (100 – 95 percent) that the relationship between training and sales happened by chance. To tie this together, we can say that "We are 95 percent confident that 60 percent (R^2) of the increase in sales is a direct result of the increase in dollars spent on training." See Appendix D for a deeper dive into regression modeling.

CASE STUDY

CHRYSLER ACADEMY, DEALERSHIP SALES CONSULTANT TRAINING, PART 2

Chrysler Academy's quest to prove the business impact of sales training started with a well-known statistic that trained sales consultants outsell their untrained counterparts by an average of 35 vehicles each year. There were several business questions Chrysler Academy wanted to answer:

- Can training claim credit for some percentage of the 35 vehicle increase in sales?
- Does training increase retention of sales consultants in a traditionally high-turnover environment?
- What is the business case for dealers to send their sales consultants to training?
- How can Chrysler Academy maximize the benefits of training?

In order to answer these business questions, the study considered three metrics:

1. New vehicle sales volume
2. Sales satisfaction scores
3. Sales consultant retention

To determine whether demographics had any influence, the study also included the following metrics:

- Dealer size.
- Franchises carried (e.g., a Chrysler dealer compared to a Chrysler-Jeep-Dodge dealer).
- Non-Chrysler franchises (e.g., a Chrysler dealer compared to a Chrysler-Subaru dealer).
- Consultant tenure.
- Sales consultant training and certification history.
- Presence of a trained sales manager.
- Manager-to-consultant ratio.
- "Fixed First Visit" score (based on surveys completed by customers following their first visit to a dealership).
- Customer satisfaction score.

(Continued)

The data for these metrics and demographics included 33,867 sales consultants and 3,000 independent dealers. Such a large sample size, although by no means required for business impact work, allowed for a very high level of statistical certainty. The dealers represented 10 dealer types and sizes. Two years' worth of data were pulled from Chrysler's learning management system (LMS), dealer personnel system, dealer financial system, customer satisfaction survey system, and new vehicle delivery system.

The first question, "Can training claim credit for some percentage of the 35 vehicle increase in sales?" required isolating the impact of training from all of the other variables affecting sales consultant sales numbers. As shown in Exhibit 6.2, by using test and control groups that accounted for fully trained, partially trained, and untrained sales consultants, the study found that 15.6 of those 35 vehicles were attributable to training.

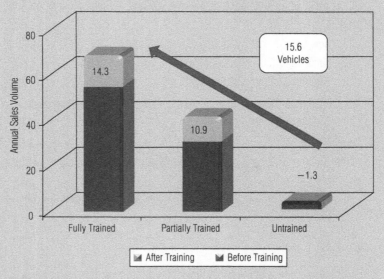

Exhibit 6.2 Isolation: Training's Impact on Sales
Reprinted with permission from Chrysler Academy

In fact, during the study period, untrained consultants actually saw a decrease in sales. The isolated impact of training on new vehicle sales volume gave Chrysler Academy evidence that training did, in fact, contribute to overall sales performance. Furthermore, the Academy could share this finding with dealers to encourage them to invest in the training. Rather than give dealers a return on investment (ROI) percentage, a rather abstract concept, the academy reported the findings in the dealers' language. Dealers could easily imagine an average of 15.6 extra vehicles driving off of their lots each year for each sales consultant they trained. That's more than one vehicle per month, per sales consultant. Because dealers are intimately familiar with the profit numbers each vehicle represents for their business, these results really hit home.

What about retention? Again, dealership sales consultants traditionally turned over at an extremely high rate. As shown in Exhibit 6.3, during the study period, only 48 percent of new sales consultants were retained for 90 days posthire (compared with a 75 percent retention rate of their untrained veteran peers). The isolated impact of training on retention (again calculated through the control and test group methodology) showed an increase to a 99 percent retention rate for fully trained sales consultants within 90 days of their hire date. Chrysler Academy was able to prove that training new hires increases their retention, thereby reducing turnover costs and increasing sales readiness.

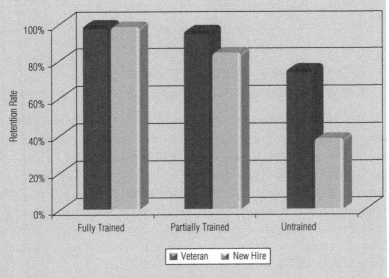

Exhibit 6.3 Training's Impact on Retention
Reprinted with permission from Chrysler Academy

SUMMARY

The quest to create "proof" of theories or validate facts has kept many philosophers and scientists busy over the years. In human capital, projects should always be an improvement in surety over what was done before. Given that, we do occasionally get to a highly satisfying proof. A very important concept to understand is that "correlation does not equal causation." In other words, just because two things co-occur does not mean one caused the other—there may be some underlying mechanism behind both of them or it could be purely coincidental.

Proving causation offers a spectrum of items to consider, because different situations call for different approaches. Here are some of the basic questions to consider when making a logical case:

- Can you separate out your participants and data into those who received the intervention (test group) and those who did not (control group)?
- Are there observable differences between the groups, more so than could be accounted for by random chance?
- Have you accounted for prior performance?
- Did you consider time-related changes?
- Did you look at the descriptive statistics?
- Have you considered the relationship between the metrics?

When your measurement map is clear, and you have identified the data required, it is time to think about the statistics involved. Statistics are about assessing whether there is an impact, and, if so, how much that impact is. Regression analysis is a common tool in the measurement of human capital. The basic idea behind regression modeling is fitting a line to a piece of data. These techniques are powerful for assessing the magnitude of an impact, creating a rigor and discipline in how to determine whether the changes are significant or just random noise, and deciding which factors drive the changes.

Our approaches typically blend equal doses of data and math with logical, convincing storytelling. Our goal is to show both how our case is logical *and* that we have quantitatively ruled out other causes. These methods, coupled with patience and clear thinking, will set you on your way to making the best possible decisions.

NOTES

1. R. W. Emerson, *The Conduct of Life: By Ralph Waldo Emerson* (Lanham, MD: University Press of America, 2006; orig. 1860).
2. W. Cascio and J. Boudreau, *Investing in People: Financial Impact of Human Resource Initiatives* (Upper Saddle River, NJ: Pearson Education, 2011).
3. P. P. Phillips and J. J. Phillips, *ROI in Action Casebook* (*Measurement and Evaluation*) (San Francisco: Pfeiffer, 2008).
4. T. Dehue, "History of the Control Group," in B. S. Everitt and D. C. Howell, *Encyclopedia of Statistics in Behavioral Science* (Chichester: John Wiley & Sons, 2005), 829–836.
5. K. Cherry, *Hawthorne Effect* (n.d.), retrieved April 16, 2012, from About .Com Psychology, http://psychology.about.com/od/hindex/g/def_hawthorn .htm.

CHAPTER 7

Beyond ROI to Optimization

"At a time when companies offer similar products and comparable technology, high-performance business processes are among the last remaining points of differentiation."

—Tom Davenport, *Competing on Analytics*[1]

A big conceptual improvement over simple measurement is provided by return on investment (ROI).[2] ROI has enabled countless trainers to demonstrate the valuable work they do in improving human capital for their organizations. Although ROI provides a valuable measure of success, we suggest going one step further. The next building block is optimization, a prescriptive analysis that identifies where investments are most needed and the intelligent allocation of those investments. ROI is sometimes criticized, not entirely fairly, for being a historical marker. It is not uncommon to find people who look at ROI only in a backward fashion—they want to clarify the value of what they have done, rather than prepare for the next year's work. It is useful to know the outcome of past work so as not to repeat the same mistakes. However, even if successful, the past is not a predictor of the future. Still, the greater value comes not from knowing the past but from being able to predict the future.

OPTIMIZATION

By understanding where the investment is working—and where it isn't—you can make targeted adjustments that improve impact over time. Optimization requires that an investment be isolated. Isolation is a historical finding, showing what has already happened. Optimization estimates how to take steps to predictively improve future outcomes, which means making changes that are certain to have greater impact.

We use the word *optimization* in several different ways, each of which implies getting more out of the data than a simple impact assessment. Optimization techniques all increase the strength of the isolation and help you understand the data in new ways.

Segmentation

Segmentation is the first key concept involved in optimization and the most likely to bear fruit. Segmentation is an analysis that breaks down the impact on a group-by-group basis to understand where the greatest and least impacts are achieved. For example, a sales training program may be successful at boosting sales overall. However, segmentation might reveal that new sales representatives receive a great lift in their performance, while seasoned representatives show little to no benefit from the training. In some cases, the effect might be negative overall, but some groups may show a benefit. In earlier chapters, we laid out some of the criteria for a good demographic variable to use in segmentation: it should have a plausible effect on the metrics of interest, it should mediate the effect of any investments, and it should be a valid criteria for decision making.

Exhibit 7.1 shows an optimization from a project involving the sales force from a $2 billion agriculture company. The sales force was heterogeneous, ranging from agents who sold the products full time to independent agents who sold their products as only one part of their offerings. Conventional wisdom suggested that the training should be prioritized for the top professionals. As part of the analysis, we looked at sales figures prior to the implementation of the training program and broke the agents into five quintiles: the bottom 20 percent, and so

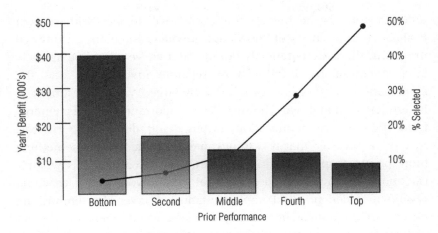

Exhibit 7.1 Optimization and the Possible Consequences

forth, up to the top 20 percent. We mainly wanted to use this information to correct for their selection bias and get a more accurate impact. What we found was far more interesting. The height of the five bars displays the difference in impact: the average improvement for the trainees, compared to the untrained group. The improvement for the (previously) underperforming quintile was almost $40,000 in extra sales per year, while the impact dollars for the original high performers was less and less, eventually dropping below $10,000. The message is clear: Train all of the low performers first! The training is still worthwhile for the top performers, but the ROI is much lower. The black line shows training rates for the five quintiles. The right-hand *y*-axis shows the percentages in each quintile selected for training. Less than 10 percent of the low performers were trained, compared to almost 50 percent for the top performers. The company was pursuing *exactly* the wrong strategy. We calculated that by using only the existing $2 million training budget, filling the classrooms with the lowest performers represented a $27 million yearly improvement in return.

Mixture

Mixture is the second key concept in optimization. Most companies are spreading their human capital investments among a number of different pots on the human resources stove. In fact, with content available from a variety of knowledge providers and many customized programs, there are potentially dozens (and we've seen, in extremely large organizations, hundreds) of separate investments, and the combinations can become astronomically large. Which investment or investments should we choose? Two important concepts emerge from the mixture optimization: synergy and diminishing returns. Synergy is the idea that two things may combine to offer something more potent than the sum of the parts. We have seen this when a classroom session provided theoretical groundwork and a coaching session provided practical implementation. Conversely, diminishing returns are programs where multiple items are combined, and the net effect is less than the sum of the parts. Diminishing returns can occur because there is only so much improvement to go around—"low-hanging fruit" may be a common benefit taken by more than one program. Another frequent occurrence is that there is overlapping content among different programs.

Saturation

Saturation is the third concept in optimization, the idea that the return on investment may not be a smooth, straightforward calculation. Analysts often act as if there is a magical straight line running through the process: For every dollar I subtract from the training budget, x amount of sales are lost, for every dollar, I add, x amount is added, and out to infinity. Getting a return may require a certain threshold of investment to show any returns at all or may drop off after a certain amount is invested. There are anecdotes about training programs that require a certain penetration before the idea can catch hold. People report returning to the workplace and finding out the new revolutionary ideas they have gotten are not welcomed. They may not be specifically discouraged; it is just that there may not be support for the ideas. Teachers have long known that some ideas are not fun or initially productive and require some level of practice or reinforcement before they become habits. The opposite phenomena may occur: an investment may be overdone. It is easy to answer the question of how productive an employee is who spends 100 percent of his or her time in training—regardless of how good the training is, the employee must have some period of time to do his or her actual work. An investment or a program that deals with handling an emerging situation or market must leave some room for old programs that deal with the status quo. Compensation is one area where saturation concepts apply. Providing people with a monetary incentive may be effective, but at what point have you reached maximum effectiveness?[3]

Metric Interaction

Metric interaction is the fourth key concept. Many analytic methods tend to focus on a single outcome. This is necessary to the extent that it simplifies the world to a version that can be analyzed. Some of the tools, such as regression models, focus on a single outcome variable in their mathematical models. It is necessary, however, to consider how the different measurements combine and interact. This is a positive attribute of the pragmatism of the ROI school of thought—it lends itself to combining and leveling variables with respect to their financial contributions.

An example where metric interaction was an important decision point was in a consumer finance setting, where call center training was being measured. The primary focus of the call center was customer service. A credit-protection program was introduced as an additional source of revenue. Training was being used to teach effective sales behavior of the customer service agents. The goal was that training programs would increase sales of the credit-protection plan, and in fact, that was the case. In addition, the training was inexpensive, and therefore the ROI on the training was quite impressive. A resounding success? Not entirely. In a routine check of those rich sets of call center metrics, the length of the call (call handle time) showed a strong correlation with both sales *and* training. Statistical techniques were used to unravel the situation. It appeared that training led to increased call handle time, and that call handle time strongly correlated with sales. That was seen as positive until the increased cost due to extra time spent was considered. Sales representatives spent a lot of the extra time selling the credit protection product, partly due to training, but mostly due to a financial incentive. However, attempts to sell the product had a fairly low success rate, and the profit margin was low. The most important question was not whether training had an impact, but whether the customer service representatives should have been selling the new product at all. The conclusion was no.

Many times, the results are surprising and counterintuitive. The previous example where training resulted in a net loss on important metrics is far from the most common type of metric interaction. Much more commonly, we see multiple positive effects from an investment. In our experience, in addition to performance improvements, training programs almost always improve retention. This should come as no surprise. People are most satisfied when they have the skills to do a good job, and a company that is succeeding is usually making employee conditions better and taking numerous other actions that make the company a better place to work.

Time Line

Time line is the fifth concept in optimization. Time lines require that we divide the data into more groups than just the traditional "before the investment" and "after the investment." Investments may be said to have varying degrees of "stickiness." A "highly sticky" investment continues to offer benefits for a long time. Other "less sticky" investments see their impact lost after a period of time. Motivational interventions, in our experience, follows the "less sticky" path. After some number of months, motivation seems to return to the baseline levels. Another example of programs that become "less sticky" over time is certain types of technical training that focus on aspects that are prone to change over time (e.g., sales training that provides training based on the current year's models; new equipment whose advantages fade as the industry standardizes to the new level of technology). The other side of "stickiness" is "lag time." Some programs may take some period of time to show their advantage. Industries with long sales cycles often experience "lag time." If a sales training program provides advantages in filling the "pipeline" for products that may take eighteen months between initial contact and closing the deal, measuring the effects after six months may lead to the wrong conclusion. In this case, you would want to measure the leading indicators, which was discussed in detail in Chapter 3.

Time line effects, in our experience, are usually difficult to find. This is due to the fact that when the data sets are sliced into smaller time periods, the lower number of data points reduces the chance of finding statistical significance.

CASE STUDY

CHRYSLER ACADEMY, DEALERSHIP SALES CONSULTANT TRAINING, PART 3

Once Chrysler Academy had isolated the impact of sales consultant training on the business, it had hard evidence of return on the investment in training to show business leadership and dealers. The next step was to optimize sales consultant training—considering where it was working best and concentrating resources in those areas.

Chrysler categorizes its dealers by five sizes: A through E, with E dealers representing the largest dealerships and A dealers being the smallest. The study found that the larger the dealership, the greater the impact of live training on sales results (see Exhibit 7.2).

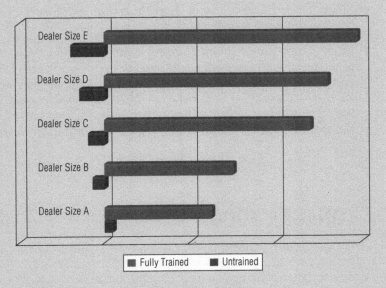

Exhibit 7.2 Live Training's Impact on Unit Sales
Reprinted with permission from Chrysler Academy

(Continued)

Live training is expensive, and Chrysler had only a limited amount of trainers qualified to deploy this training. This finding pointed to an opportunity to send these scarce resources to the dealerships where they would generate the greatest impact on sales (larger dealers) and where to use other training modalities (such as e-learning) with the smaller dealers.

The basic "case study" impact provides only a flavor of the amount of information that can be gleaned from a data set that contains dozens of variables, performance reports, training materials, and strategic reports. Working with Chrysler allowed us to understand its company culture and address specific questions circulating within the organization, related to the applicability of training to different sizes and types of dealerships, different geographic regions, and different types of workers. We were able to analyze modalities of training, certification programs, the interaction of manager training with consultant training, and many other areas of human capital development. A great project does not usually come to an end after the initial analysis. Rather, it is more like the opening of a gold mine that continues to provide a wealth of information and benefit to the company.

By optimizing the impact of sales consultant training, Chrysler Academy could continue to show hard evidence of its contributions and improve the business performance. The academy was also armed with valuable information when marketing training to the dealers who pay for these services. Finally, the optimization process was able to guide future changes in the content of the sales consultant curriculum and for measuring the business impact of those changes. Chrysler provided us with an excellent opportunity to share information with diverse stakeholders within the organization. For example, some dealerships believed that training was a zero-sum game, with trained consultants taking a larger share of a fixed number of sales and leaving the dealership unchanged after training expenses were met. We were able to specifically refute this myth, removing a cultural obstacle to effective training.

CONAGRA FOODS

CASE STUDY

ConAgra Foods is a leading producer of nationally known food brands, including Healthy Choice, Chef Boyardee, Hunts, Orville Redenbacher, Hebrew National, and many others. Their brands can be found in 97 percent of U.S. households.

In 2008, ConAgra Foods underwent dramatic changes, selling several operations to focus exclusively on packaged foods. As the company became

"One ConAgra," it launched Foundations of Leadership, a three-tier, multiyear curriculum to cultivate leaders aligned with the new corporate vision. Leaders at all levels wanted to better understand the impact of this investment.

Stakeholders gathered in August 2009 to identify the scope of the study and business performance indicators. Consumer and commercial plant operations, marketing leadership, legal, human resources, and organizational development were represented. The stakeholders determined that the study would specifically look at trained and untrained front-line plant supervisors to determine impact on leader retention, leader mobility, plant productivity, plant quality, and plant safety. Capital Analytics included other factors in the evaluation to determine whether such things as plant size and a leader's tenure with the company were influencing those metrics.

The program was piloted in February 2008 and launched worldwide in May of the same year. The course was offered monthly to front-line supervisors, and the business impact study analyzed the performance of 600 trained and 1,600 untrained supervisors. ConAgra determined that the study would cover a subset of 65 U.S.-based plants. The plants employed a range of 6 to 1,440 employees. Data were collected from each plant. Some of the data were descriptive, for example, plant size (number of employees), segment, platform (consumer vs. commercial foods), and plant manager. Consumer food was further analyzed by frozen, grocery, refrigerated, and snacks. Business impact was analyzed on both a plant and an individual basis.

To completely explore the impact of training, statistical models looked at the combination of plant size and training penetration to evaluate the interaction of these variables as they relate to plant metrics.

During the 12-month period under study, overall turnover of supervisors did drop significantly—from 12.7 to 9.4 percent. But was this attributable to the training?

Further examination confirmed that turnover among trained supervisors was 6.1 percentage points lower than for untrained supervisors—a value of $2.3 million in year one alone (see Exhibit 7.3).

In assessing the training's impact on safety, a clear difference was established between small and large plants. Small plants with "high" training penetration levels saw a 1.55 point increase on a 10-point scale. However, large plants with the same training level saw only a 0.2 point increase, highlighting the opportunity to seek other safety-improvement interventions in these environments (see Exhibit 7.4).

(Continued)

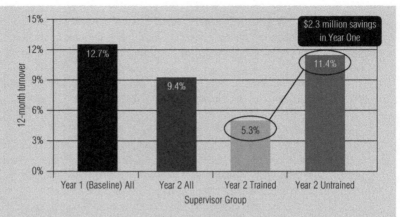

Exhibit 7.3   12-Month Turnover of Supervisors
Reprinted with permission from ConAgra

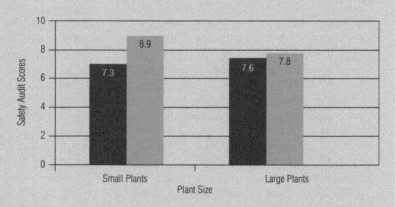

Exhibit 7.4   Impact of Training on Safety Audit Scores
Reprinted with permission from ConAgra

In addition, trained supervisors were more than 1.5 times more likely to be promoted as untrained supervisors.

Summary

Foundations of Leadership generated a significant, positive ROI and created a leadership foundation for the future. Not only were trained supervisors more likely to be promoted, but they were more likely to stay with the organization and drive meaningful performance within their work units as well. Based on hard data, ConAgra leaders were able to make confident decisions on fine-tuning future training deployment.

SUMMARY

Optimization is the next level beyond business impact and ROI. In this chapter, we included a number of concepts that involve breaking down the impact to find out where, when, and for whom the impact occurs. This allows future investments to be done prescriptively, rather than retroactively. Optimization requires more and better data and of the sort we describe in Chapter 5 on descriptive statistics. Extra data not only improve the certainty and accuracy of the impact assessment but also provide all of the extra optimization information. The main aspects of optimization are

- **Segmentation** is dividing up impact based on demographic or other categorical data, to determine how the different groups respond to the investment.

- **Mixture** is breaking down complex programs into multiple parts, to find out which programs have the best ROI and how they combine to provide potential synergies and diminishing returns.

- **Saturation** looks at the amount of training in an organization or for an individual, to find whether there is a "tipping point" or threshold that needs to be crossed before the return is realized. Conversely, saturation also asks whether there is a point where adding to the training investment will lead to diminishing returns.

- **Metric interaction** tests the relationship between the key performance indicators. Several outcomes are possible, both positive and negative. First, there may be a tradeoff where a positive return in one area is counterbalanced by a loss in another area. Second and most common, multiple positive effects are seen in several areas.

■ **Time lines** are an examination of how performance changes over time. Programs may require some "latency" time to kick in or may fade over time.

Optimization is the key selling point for the use of more complex analysis. It moves us from simple "measuring an investment" to actually improving future work.

NOTES

1. Tom Davenport, *Competing on Analytics: The New Science of Winning* (Cambridge, MA: Harvard Business School Press, 2007).
2. J. J. Phillips, *Return on Investment in Training and Performance Improvement Programs* (Houston: Gulf Publishing Company, 1997).
3. Dan Ariely, *Predictably Irrational: The Hidden Forces That Shape Our Decisions* (New York: HarperCollins Publishers, 2008).

CHAPTER **8**

Share the Story

"Simplicity is the ultimate sophistication."

—Leonardo da Vinci

"Make it as simple as possible. But no simpler."

—Albert Einstein

W
ell, congratulations. You have now designed a study, gathered all of the disparate data, and run the statistical modeling, and you have a pile of results that is more or less interesting. There are actionable results in here, but it still may be pretty complicated. So how do you work with them? The final part of the job will be communicating results around the organization. You should already have some ideas about possible plans of action, especially if you followed our advice in the earlier chapters. We compare the development of an action plan early to "follow-through" on a golf or tennis ball. It should be part of one continuous smooth motion that consistently aims for the right spot.

First, consider what documents you need to deliver. We use a "spearhead" approach, as shown in Exhibit 8.1.

The elevator pitch is exactly that: A concise statement of what was learned from the analysis, short enough to be delivered during an elevator ride.

The executive summary is a brief document that tells the "story" of the study, focusing mostly on the impact of the results and the

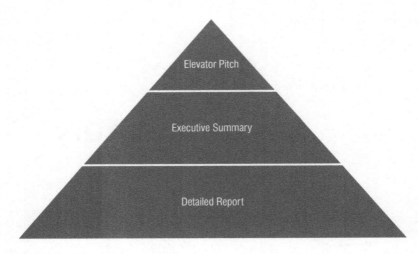

Exhibit 8.1 Spearhead Approach

optimization steps recommended for improvement. It is written at a memo level (i.e., what an executive needs to know about the project). Generally, this report is two to three pages. Even though it can be very difficult to edit the range of results in complicated projects, we suggest keeping the executive summary in this circumstance down to five or six pages. This report is accompanied by a slide deck, highlighting the major sections from the executive summary. It may even be condensed down into a handful of slides.

The detailed report lays out what happened in the project: where the data came from, what assumptions were made, detailed breakdowns of the data by demographics, and what statistical models were built.

During many years of doing these projects, we have despaired at the realization that a majority of people in the corporate world don't like to read. Those detailed reports are rarely read. So why do we write them? Granted, some clients really do dig down into the details, but partly it's for us, because some of the interesting results have a way of circulating around the organization for months or years. So, later, we have had people come back and want to know exactly how a particular conclusion was reached, what set of employees was the study group, or whether a particular factor was controlled. This might happen when a major related investment is being contemplated or when the work is being put forward for an award or a presentation.

It used to bother us more that the detailed reports weren't being read, but given the size of the organizations we work for, sometimes a couple of slides take on a life of their own and move around the organization, actually changing policy. That is where decisions are made. One of the authors recalls going to colloquia in graduate school, where an hour's detailed presentation on research would create virtually no lasting impression. By mid-afternoon, only the general topic could be recalled; the conclusion, the methods, and the takeaway message had long evaporated, due to confusing presentation style, overload, and poor messaging. If an executive can carry away from your project enough important conclusions to fill a Post-it note and remember them and take action on them, you have done a great job, and all of that time will have been worthwhile.

First and foremost, speak the language of business. Translate the statistical "gobbledygook" into business terms, and drop any HR speak. Present findings simply and clearly. Use charts to show complex data, while avoiding big tables.

Remember to ask yourself whose story you are telling. One common problem with reports is the tendency to tell the story from your perspective—where the data came from, how you filtered the numbers, why you are solving the problem, what analysis methods you used, and so forth. Sadly, most people don't care. Talk in terms of the benefits to their business. If there are some powerful business results that are going to affect policy, put them right up front. If the readers have to get through the historical preliminaries, you will often lose their attention by the time the important stuff comes up.

PRESENTING THE FINANCIALS

We do not have a hard-and-fast rule for presenting financials, other than "know your audience." Some companies really like things condensed down to an ROI percentage, and others like to have more of the basic impact. Working with Chrysler, we were advised not to provide outcomes in terms of ROI—everyone thinks and talks in terms of new vehicle units sold, so that's the currency. One person told us, "ROI is just a number. When you tell me 15 cars, I can look out my window and see that."

Most organizations will have some financial numbers for which they have buy-in across the organization. These numbers will be very useful. Average, fully loaded hourly cost of an employee is one of those. A good estimate for replacing a lost employee is another.

Jack and Patti Phillips, the experts on ROI, repeatedly advise to *be conservative* when making financial reports. This is great advice.[1] Nothing will derail the confidence of the audience faster than a greedy financial assumption. Over the years, it has been a rare occasion that anyone wants to question the more sophisticated mathematical analyses we do. Yet it is common for people to ask for clarification about something, such as the percentage of sales revenue that is profit, for example. If you have a range of values into which the number might fall, always pick the conservative end of the range. Remember, the financial assumptions should have been agreed to in the design of the study, up front, so that they don't become an issue after the study is conducted.

In practice, there may be a spectrum between business impact in units and a full ROI percentage. You may just wish to present a handful of the values and allow the audience members to draw their own conclusions. Remember that in most cases, you are going to be talking about both returns and costs.

There are a number of variations on ROI: net present value, cost-benefit ratios, and others. Your stakeholders should include members of the financial unit; inquire about their expectations. What time periods are they comfortable using? Are they focusing on cost-cutting or revenue enhancement measures? Is risk mitigation important? A good book that walks the L&D professional through accounting conventions from an ROI perspective is *Quick! Show Me Your Value.*[2]

TELLING THE STORY AND ADDING UP THE NUMBERS

We recommend using a variety of data to tell your story, if is available. The most important information is the business impact, told from the standpoint of the operational data, and, of course, how you believe it can be improved, using optimization. Long-term experience teaches us to simplify the story, starting at 50,000 feet and spiraling in from there. Interest in this work is growing within HR. Most likely, several people in your audience love numbers and will eagerly consume them, but how will you get through to people who fear numbers? Look back at the continuum of measurement, as shown in Chapter 1. Anecdotes or hero stories are great techniques to add color, comfort, and credibility. We try to add a compelling quote or two, early on in the executive summary. Have you ever been to Disney World? The parking lots are identified by a number, a color, and a Disney character. The idea is that you could use several different unique identifiers, so people have several different ways in which to remember where they parked their cars. You might emulate this in presenting several different kinds of data that all point toward the same general conclusion.

Graphics are a great tool for enhancing clarity and visually displaying the results of your analysis. We recommend graphics that tell the readers things that they would have difficulty figuring out from a table of data. Graphics will show you that the eye is a great statistician—concepts such as effect size, statistical certainty, and variance may be difficult to explain mathematically, but when displayed graphically, these concepts may appear obvious to the reader without your even having to explain them.

Graphics can bring your concepts to life. Some great resources for examples include videos made by Hans Rosling for the TED conference on global health that make complex numbers come to life.[3] Or pick up one of Edward Tufte's elegant books on graphic design and presentation.[4]

Exhibits 8.2 and 8.3 are graphs with important lessons. The bar chart in Exhibit 8.2 shows that training lowered turnover the greatest among employees with less than one year tenure. Notice how we were not shy to add a circle on the figure to emphasize the important message.

Scatterplots display both the amount and the spread of the data. In Exhibit 8.3, the trend line shows how manufacturing rates slightly improve as a result of training saturation in the plant. Because the slope of the line is very subtle, the trend line helps display the effect. This is important because even with the small increase, the improvements are valued in the millions of dollars.

In Exhibit 8.4, we see a comparison of the populations between "All Employees" and "Employee Users" across different business

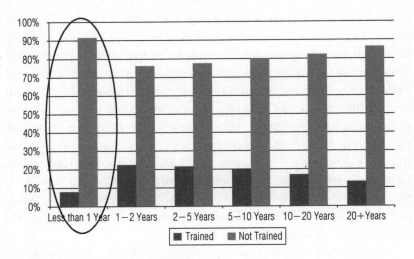

Exhibit 8.2 Training by Tenure; Supply Chain—Consumer

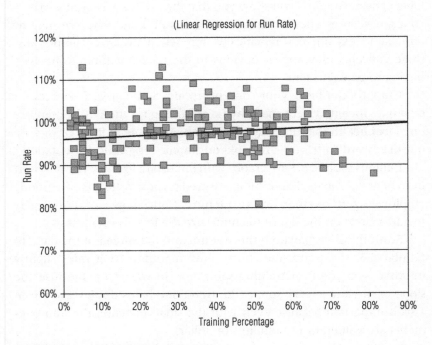

Exhibit 8.3 Training's Impact on Run Rate

categories. Notice how the categories are ordered to show a comparison as the population for "All Employees" declines. This is a great technique to visually enhance your story.

Exhibit 8.5 makes a couple of important points. First, it tells the story over time. Stakeholders typically want to know how things

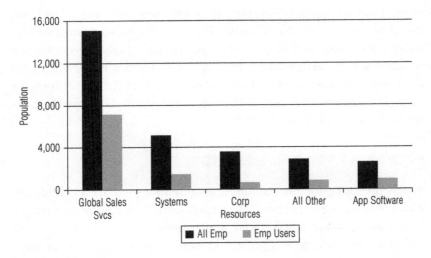

Exhibit 8.4 Bar Chart Example

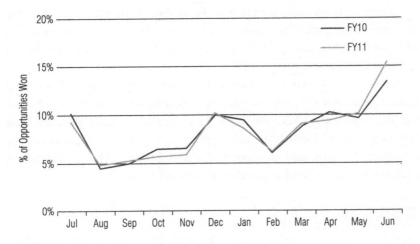

Exhibit 8.5 Line Chart with a Categorical Overlay

changed and evolved during certain time periods. Second, by over-laying the data in the same graph, comparisons of different categories become much easier. In this graph, the two financial years are superimposed to compare "Opportunities Won" over their yearly cycles.

Graphics can be one of your more important tools. Use them, but don't overuse them. Consider the colors you are using, and ask whether they can be distinguished if the reader is color-blind (or, far more commonly, is using a noncolor printer). Make sure that the graphics are understandable, the legends and scales make sense and are honest representations of the impact, and that the graph contains enough unique information that it can be identified if it moves from its original location in the document.

PREPARING FOR THE MEETINGS

When preparing for the meetings, assume that your stakeholders are going to ask tough questions. Anticipating those questions in advance is crucial. Finding someone to walk through the reports and ask questions in advance is a great first step. Some of the most popular questions are in the areas of headcount and finance. Sometimes, the easiest questions can trip you up.

Keep your message simple and direct. We often make up slides for the most anticipated questions. We include them in the appendix of our presentation so that we can easily gain access to them when a question arises.

If someone is very challenging, especially around the analytics, we have found that this person has the potential to become one of your biggest supporters. Spending the time to share your approach and techniques is well worth the effort. Because what you are presenting is complex thinking and analytical decision making, this individual is inclined to understand and value your work.

SUMMARY

All of the good work you have done so far is important, and you deserve a pat on the back. The goal is to make a case for changes to corporate policy that will improve business outcomes. Ultimately, the results of projects with hundreds of statistical models are often summarized into a slide or two of important, eye-catching details. Those are the slides that are circulated at the highest levels. They need to carry the impact of the project. We use a set of tiers, starting with the short elevator pitch, writing a few pages of executive summary, and then the more detailed report. If your work has the impact you desire, the detailed report will help you answer any specific questions that arise. On occasion, our work has inspired questions from within high levels of the organization more than a year later.

Your reports should tell readers *what they need to know first*. Talk about the project history and the challenges and sources of the data only at a later time, if necessary. Often, there is a strong tendency to tell your story first and the data's story second, but the best results are seen when the story focuses on the benefits to the company. All good salespeople know to focus on benefits over features.

Your report should be in plain English. Avoid any HR and statistical terminology. We have included a glossary in the back of the book that may prove useful in figuring out how to restate your information. The graphics are an important part of your storytelling. Graphics offer several formats and range from simple to complex. We like to say that the eye is a good statistician. A well-chosen graph can get across concepts of statistically significant impact without any exchange of words.

NOTES

1. P. Phillips, "Show Me the Money: Moving from Impact to ROI. Measuring ROI for People, Projects, and Programs," American Society for Training and Development conference, Atlanta, GA, June 2007.
2. T. Seagraves, *Quick! Show Me Your Value* (Alexandria, VA: ASTD Press, 2004).
3. H. Rosling, "Hans Rosling Shows You the Best Stats You've Ever Seen," June 2007, retrieved June 13, 2012, from TED.com, www.ted.com/talks/hans_rosling_shows_the_best_stats_you_ve_ever_seen.html.
4. E. R. Tufte, *The Visual Display of Quantitative Information* (Cheshire, CT: Graphics Press, 2001).

CHAPTER **9**

Conclusion

A t the beginning of the book, we stated that HR practitioners have begun to embrace analytics at the same time that organizational leaders are demanding increasing accountability from HR. We now know that analytics has greatly improved our ability to measure the results of human capital investments through the methods and the case studies described in this book. Analytics is a complex science. When we apply it to human behavior in organizational settings, it becomes even more complex. Yet the joy of analytics is that it opens one's eyes to a vast landscape of possibilities and that, when applied successfully, it allows for amazing insights.

Analytics promises to describe, with a high degree of probability, the behavior of people inside organizations. Now we are able to apply descriptive analytics to understand current human capital problems and prescriptive analytics to improve future outcomes from human capital investments.

Descriptive analytics tells what has happened in the past and often unveils the cause of the outcome. Predictive analytics uses past behavior to predict future outcomes, telling what is likely to happen given a stated approach. Predictive analytics requires a more sophisticated understanding of what variables we know to be correlated and when we can develop a stronger case, an argument for causation. Knowing enough about your data to argue for causation usually provides enough information to optimize your investment—understanding for whom, when, and where those investments will work the best.

The good news is that the human resources profession is waking up to the potential value of analysis, particularly predictive analytics. Ultimately, our goal is to invest more wisely in human capital for the good of the people, as well as for the benefit to the organization at large.

HUMAN CAPITAL ANALYTICS

Human capital is the most important differentiator of a modern company. We are at a moment in time where theories about human capital, the amount of data available, and the computing power necessary to deal with the data are radically changing how business is done. Today organizations are at different levels on the analytics continuum (see Chapter 1). All of analytics are useful: We collect data that range from anecdotes to hard operational data interpreted with statistics. Anecdotes add stories and context to your reports. The rigorous analysis that provides true insight and helps you optimize your investments for maximum impact is the most important goal in the management of human capital. It is absolutely necessary to ensure your company's success in this new century.

Lowe's accomplished that level of analysis, as described in the case study in Chapter 1. For many organizations, integrating HR, customer, operations, financial, and other types of data can be daunting. Barriers to conducting this type of analysis were overcome at Lowe's, and it developed a methodology designed specifically to measure the relationships of HR data points to other metrics throughout the organization. Today, Lowe's has captured the impact of employee attitudes and how this affects the business—this is a milestone step for the HR business function. Lowe's is beginning to translate these models into forward-looking, predictive analytics.

ALIGNMENT

Alignment is a plan that explicitly connects investments to strategic goals via the metrics. Alignment is about finding the relevant stakeholders in the company and connecting them to the parts in that plan. Alignment enables you to measure and improve the investment's impact and positions human resources as a strategic partner in support of the business.

The alignment process outlined in Chapter 2 involves defining success for an investment, gaining stakeholder buy-in to the indicators of success, and ensuring that success is measurable. You must find out who your stakeholders are, create the right environment and tools to align the stakeholders, the metrics, the strategic goals, and the investments. The alignment process does not go deep into the data, but it creates a shared vision of what needs to be measured. Knowing and agreeing upon what needs to be measured is a profound way to create alignment among your stakeholders.

In Chapter 2, Rio Tinto showed the power of designing an alignment process to its contractor management system. After a successful pilot program, the solution has now been adopted as a global standard and is being deployed around the world.

Rio Tinto discovered a number of lessons learned in how to manage change in a business:

- Ensure that the data analysis leads to the identification of the root cause of the problem with face validity.
- Select an issue that is a core driver for the company and is in alignment with culture and values.
- Work cross-functionally to create synergy and ensure full support for solution development and implementation.
- Design the solution in conjunction with the business to ensure adoption and minimize resistance.
- Adequately resource the project at every level, from conception to final review and implementation.

THE MEASUREMENT PLAN

Once you have completed the process of alignment with your stakeholders, you are ready to design an action plan for measuring your investment. A good practice is to pull together your measurement plan directly following the stakeholder meeting, and offer to review it with any interested stakeholders. If your study includes a group of interventions, be sure to clearly define what is and is not included. You may also want to consider selecting a subset of interventions that is representative of a larger program.

A complete measurement plan has several major components. It identifies the business questions in a specific way and defines the metrics, the investments, and the participants. You should end up with a measurement map and a listing of the data sources and your expectations of them.

A measurement map is a visual depiction of the alignment between an investment and the organization's strategic goals (see Exhibit 9.1). The map provides the measurable links that form the basis of your study by using business metrics to show the logical relationships between the investment and goals. The measurement map's leading indicators and business results will typically map to your metrics. Once the metrics and the demographics for the study have been established, you are ready to tackle the data sources and requirements.

Sun Microsystems showed in Chapter 3 how measurement plans align HR investments with business outcomes. Sun's 's learning and development work was about creating a clear line of sight between investments and business goals. By applying a systematic approach to this

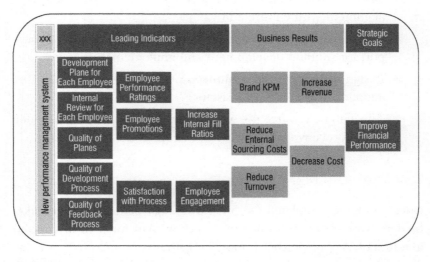

Exhibit 9.1 Measurement Map

line of sight to its new social learning platform, Sun was able to understand who was using the new platform, what groups were creating new content, and which content was highly rated and consumed. It could track the usage between informal and formal learning and begin to understand the tanagible and intangible benefits of this new investment.

IT'S ALL ABOUT THE DATA

For a successful measurement initiative, you will want to draw data from systems inside and outside the HR organization. You will often be pulling operational data from a variety of types of systems, such as sales or operations. Your core data will come from human resource information systems (HRIS), and also learning management systems (LMS), which contain information about training. Social media and informal learning systems are becoming more and more important. Engagement surveys are effective instruments for gauging sentiment by employees. Sometimes interviewing is a good way to understand a business process before a more rigorous analysis can be undertaken. Given the sensitive nature of the personnel data, measurement and evaluation efforts require that the team and the stakeholders adopt a code of ethics and principles.

In Chapter 4, U.S. Bank illustrated how the detailed organization of data required to do an analysis provides a road map for targeting and further improving the business impact of future training interventions and redesigns—feedback on innovation so often requested by higher management.

U.S. Bank's Branch Manager Toolbook was a self-directed learning program designed to help branch managers and assistant branch managers be more effective in their leadership roles at the bank branch level. By stratifying the original data between such key factors as tenure and prior branch performance, the training organization had useful details to make targeted recommendations to upper management.

WHAT DASHBOARDS ARE TELLING YOU: DESCRIPTIVE STATISTICS AND CORRELATIONS

Today, most HR organizations have some method of reporting data on their activities. These methods can be as simple as an Excel spreadsheet kept on a user's desktop or may involve specialized or custom-written tools for databases or business intelligence. The reports that come out of these data sources are descriptive statistics. The idea of a descriptive statistic is to provide a quick indicator of what is going in the organization, such as: What is the headcount? Who completed what training? How much is payroll? The information from these sources would generally be presented in some kind of dashboard and/or scorecard.

Descriptive statistics are the foundation of your analytics efforts. Combining different data sets together produces intelligence synergies. You can discover things in the organizations that might have previously gone unnoticed. A very small amount of math and graphical representation will go a long, long way in helping you understand your business structure and processes.

Correlations appear when various key performance indictors tend to vary in relationship to one another or other characteristics. Much of the data found in dashboards would be correlated, so it is good to use common sense and avoid making decisions on future investments based solely on correlations. Remember the story in Chapter 5 about the more ice cream we consume, the more drownings increase?

Chrysler Academy knew that trained sales consultants outsold their untrained counterparts by 35 vehicles per year, but no one had been able to establish a causal link proving that training was the factor responsible for those 35 vehicles (as opposed to other factors driving individual and business performance). Marketing touted exciting ads, product development bragged about its cool new jeeps, and the credit group boasted of attractive financing packages for driving vehicle sales.

Chrysler's dealers are Chrysler Academy's customers and pay to send their sales consultants to training. Due to high turnover of new sales consultants, dealers were reluctant to send their consultants to training until they had proved they would stick around. The academy postulated that lack of training was correlated with high turnover, but once again, it had no conclusive proof to negotiate with the dealers.

These correlated metrics, both hot-button issues for Chrysler Academy, helped identify areas for further exploration. The academy could not make decisions or show proof of impact based on correlations alone, but it could begin to dig into what was happening in the field and determine the role that training played in driving sales consultants' performance and turnover.

Also in Chapter 5, VF Corporation launched Maximizing Performance, a company-wide performance management process, to support its goal of building a culture of performance and to improve business results. By deploying a variety of data-gathering techniques, VF gained the knowledge that engaged managers are essential to the development of a high-performance culture. Engaged managers encourage their associates to participate in their own professional development process. Explicitly showing employees how they contribute to the company's goals is improving engagement at VF and fostering a high-performance culture.

CAUSATION: WHAT REALLY DRIVES PERFORMANCE

The first important step to understanding performance is looking at the data and finding what patterns underlie your business. There will be both obvious conclusions and real surprises as you look at how the metrics fluctuate by region, by employee tenure, and by business unit. Don't stop with the correlations, find out how the metrics move together. Do they rise and fall together, show an inverse relationship, or have no relationship at all? These are the foundations for your analysis efforts. You can't stop at this stage, which we call correlations, however, because there is real possibility for confusion and mistaken conclusions. Doing good correlational analysis and especially moving beyond correlation to more rigorous, scientific research requires two sets of tools.

The first tool is clear logical thinking. Investigate whether you can separate your data into sets that can be called "test" and "control" groups. If participants who received some investments improved, and those who didn't get the benefit stayed the same, you have the beginnings of a proof. As Boudreau points out, you must "rule out all other possible causes," and there are many possible causes, ranging from selection bias to overzealous analytics errors, to changes over time.[1] Take some time to review some of the ways analytic efforts can go awry, and do your best to correct them.

The second tool is the programming and statistical work required for a thorough analysis, and these are as important as the first. In Chapter 6, we reviewed the ideas of statistical certainty and impact and shared a basic technique called regression modeling. Our intent was not to write a statistics text, because there are already plenty of those, but to give you the background to speak intelligently with a statistician or at least point you toward some useful starting points. Statistics can give you the degree of certainty you require in figuring out whether given factors make a difference, can distinguish between the relative contribution of those factors, and can give you some ways to estimate impact.

Continuing the Chrysler story in Chapter 6, the academy couldn't make decisions or show proof of impact based on correlations alone, but it could begin to dig into what was happening in the field and determine the role that training played in driving sales consultants' performance and turnover.

Answering "Can training claim credit for some percentage of the 35 vehicle increase in sales?" required isolating the impact of training from all of the other variables impacting sales consultants' sales numbers. By using test and control groups that accounted for fully trained, partially trained, and untrained sales consultants, the study found that on the average, 15.6 of those 35 vehicles were directly attributable to training. The isolated impact of training on new vehicle sales volume gave Chrysler Academy evidence that training did, in fact, significantly contribute to overall sales performance.

Chrysler Academy could continue to show hard evidence of its contributions to business performance. The academy was also armed with valuable information when marketing training to the dealers who pay for these services.

BEYOND ROI TO OPTIMIZATION

You don't look at your customers as a single, undifferentiated mass, so why should you look at your employees that way? The truth is, to give an accurate assessment of impact of a program, you *need* to have information at a high level of detail: How long have the employees been there? For which business units do they work? What levels of training and certification do they have? When you understand this information, you need to start applying it to the measurement of your metrics and any investments involved.

There are several different ways in which optimizations can happen. *Segmentation* is the detection of impact in different places in your organization, based on demographics such as tenure or business unit. Segmentation allows you to target current investments to where they are most effective and develop new investments to address the needs of those areas where performance is not improving. *Mixture* recognizes and reacts to the diverse set of investments many companies use to improve performance. Of the available investments, how do they stack up head-to-head, and how do they combine to create effects? *Saturation* asks whether there are inflection points in the amount of an investment you provide. Is there some threshold that needs to be reached before the results begin to appear? Is there a level of "too much" investment, where the return disappears? In short, where is the point of diminishing returns? *Metric interaction* requires that you consider how the different metrics combine. It is natural to focus on one effect at a time, but that sometimes obscures what's really happening in your organization. *Time lines* recognize that the world is more complicated than "before and after." Some investments take some time to show results; others show a spectacular early result and then fade abruptly.

The use of optimization enables the single biggest improvement in the analysis of human capital investments.

In Chapter 7, we continued the Chrysler Academy story from Chapters 5 and 6. Chrysler had isolated the impact of sales consultant training; it had hard evidence of return on the investment in training to show business leadership and dealers. The next step was to optimize sales consultant training—considering where it was working best and concentrating resources in those areas. The study found that the larger the dealership, the greater the impact of live training on sales results. Live training is expensive, and Chrysler had only a limited amount of trainers qualified to deploy this training. This finding pointed to an opportunity to send these scarce resources to the dealerships where they would generate the greatest impact on sales (larger dealers) and where to use other training modalities (such as e-learning) with the smaller dealers.

You also saw in Chapter 7 how ConAgra Foods underwent dramatic changes and launched Foundations of Leadership, a three-tier, multiyear curriculum to cultivate leaders aligned with the new corporate vision. To evaluate the business impact of the program, the study specifically looked at trained and untrained front-line plant supervisors to determine impact on leader retention, leader mobility, and plant productivity metrics. Included in the evaluation were other factors to determine whether such things as plant size and a leader's tenure with the company were influencing those metrics.

The ConAgra case study could show proof that by isolating the program from everything else, turnover among trained supervisors was 6.1 percentage points lower than for untrained supervisors—a value of $2.3 million in reduced turnover costs in Year One alone. The results of the study also directed ConAgra to select the next round of its less tenured supervisors for training, gaining maximum plant productivity and maximum retention improvement. Armed with this information, ConAgra was able to improve the results in this program for Years Two and Three of deployment.

THE ULTIMATE GOAL

The goal of this rigorous work is to present credible evidence to be able to change policy in order to improve business outcomes. The clearer and simpler you make the case, the more you will increase your chances of being persuasive. We deliver our findings in a set of tiers, starting with the short elevator pitch, writing a few pages of executive summary, then moving on to a more detailed report. Reports should be written in business language, avoiding any HR or statistical terminology. Graphics can help to communicate complex information. A relevant and well-placed anecdote can add clarity, and sometimes humor, to your presentation.

WHAT OTHERS THINK ABOUT THE FUTURE
OF ANALYTICS

Peter Drucker introduced us to the Age of Discontinuity 40 years ago. Clay Christensen taught us about the effects of disruptive technology more than 10 years ago. Most recently, Steve Jobs showed us how to leap boundaries and see things quite differently. It all boils down to an unknowable but terribly exciting world. In 1931, the Dick Tracy comic strip appeared for the first time in the *Detroit Mirror* and quickly became nationally syndicated. In 1946, Tracy's creator, Chester Gould, gave Tracy a 2-Way Wrist Radio. Readers marveled at the concept: a radio small enough to wear on your wrist. In 1964, he upgraded it to a 2-Way Television. Recently, we read about Nokia's new patent. It is for a tattoo made of ferromagnetic powder that would buzz when someone is calling. It would let the user know the caller's identity (perhaps with varying sequences of pulses). It could be placed any-where on the body. How long before the flight attendant asks us to turn off our tattoos?

This is a rapidly changing world we live and work in. Massive changes are occurring in our workforces. Technology advances have resulted in an overwhelming amount of data. Unpredictability is the new norm. Change is the new normal. We have tried to show how to improve predictability through analytic models and techniques. We hope we were successful.

Now that you have read our book or skipped directly to this section without reading a single word, it seems only fair to learn how others see the future of analytics. Dr. Jac asked some knowledgeable pro-fessional friends to give us their views on what analytics might look like 10 years from now. The following are the most insightful responses received:

> A two-day meeting hosted by a major HR vendor asked, "What's the future of strategic human capital management analytics. What will it look like? And who will own it?"
> The overwhelming consensus:
>
> ■ It will require a true set of products that measurably link to the business, that are business/finance reports, not HR reports.
>
> ■ This function will be mass adapted by business lea-ders when these solutions mature and become more business relevant.
>
> ■ HR knows too little of the business, so in 80 percent of the cases, this will reside in strategic business or finance departments.

■ With the advancements of HR outsourced transac-
tional solutions, HR in most cases will end up as a
policy and employee relations function.
—Dan Hilbert, Orca Eyes

Quite simply, analytics is the future. Organizations are
awash in a sea of data. The ones that will rise above and
achieve competitive advantage will ride the analytics wave.
They will demonstrate relationships that make the
organization more efficient and effective, and they will
create predictive models that forecast optimized
performance. Organizations that do not leverage analytics
will be washed away in the tide—fail or be acquired. The
best indicator of this trend is IBM. In the last five years, it
has purchased Cognos and SPSS—very powerful data
analytic tools. Moreover, the new CEO, Virginia Rometty,
has publicly stated that IBM's future success rests with
analytics.
—John Mattox, KnowledgeAdvisors

The issue, as I see it, is one of maturation/transformation
and not of technical/statistical innovation. The vast majority
of the people who self-select for a career in HR are not
inclined to embrace analytical thinking. They will need
to change their fundamental view of the discipline from a
transaction one to a strategic one. If we don't infuse
the function with new skills and knowledge, other
forward-looking functions such as business
planning will pick up the torch and bring it to the
corporation.
—Bob Farrell, Rio Tinto

Workforce analytics is not a fad. Speaking from watching
HR technologies through the lens of the CedarCrestone
survey for 15 years now, where we've tracked this
since 2000, this is not a fad! Neither is it mainstream, and
we have a ways to go to mature adoption. It is
definitely growing, yet way too slowly, given the
sophistication of the definers and the technologies now
available. My only worry is that the new phrase "big data"
may cloud the water for a bit while HR people figure
out what *that* means and confuse it with workforce
analytics.
—Lexi Martin, CedarCrestone

Analytics will never go away and will always be improving since it helps document impact and direct resources. Here are some challenges looking ahead. First, predictive analytics: Dashboards about the past or present need to be supplemented with insights about the future. Second, measure what is right, not what is easy. I think the right stuff, without great measures, is organization capabilities. These include measures of collaboration, speed, service, innovation, leadership brand, risk management, social responsibility, culture, and so on. Third, focus on decisions, not on data. I see too much data collected and not used to improve the quality of decisions. Start with the decisions that need to be made, and then find good data to improve the quality of the decision.

—Dave Ulrich, University of Michigan, the RBL Group

Many companies cite the importance of their human capital and its potential value as a competitive differentiator, yet the goal of maximizing human capital for most has been elusive. This despite the fact that the breadth and depth of people data have never been greater, and, with the advent of social networking, the potential of targeting specific audiences is providing a level of granularity never before achieved. Unless an organization applies analytics to this mass of human capital data, that potential is lost. Analytics allows a company's leadership to focus on the human capital barriers that are impeding its efforts in achieving its business goals. Analytics as applied to a company's human capital isn't a passing fad, since only those firms who truly maximize its human capital will achieve the competitive advantage to compete in an increasing tough, global business environment in the twenty-first century.

—Wayne Keegan, Ingram Content Group

I recently read that only eight years ago (in September 2004), a Google search for the word *podcast* returned only 526 items. This year, an estimated 40 million podcasts will be produced. So, what will HR analytics look like in 10 years? Given the pace of change today, it's obviously a little dangerous to speculate. I think the question needs to be considered in the broader context of changes that will likely occur in the workplace and how work is performed. If one looks out on a linear trajectory, it's pretty easy to think that in 10 years, "big data" will allow employers to have fully integrated employee data, from recruitment to retirement, that provides real-time feedback. But the world isn't linear. Two forces may play a significant role in how this plays out in the next decade: (1) the growing amount of project-based work being performed by a contingent and free-agent workforce, and (2) privacy. Free-agent workers may collect and maintain their own performance data or use an independent data broker to collect and validate their performance. It is inevitable that companies will be more sophisticated and adept at gathering and analyzing big data in 10 years. But with a contingent workforce, they may be more interested in the data that comes with their just-in-time workers than in the data they have in their own databases.

—Ryan Johnson, Worldatwork

For organizations to survive in today's high-tech, dynamic, global economy, they must employ and nurture a highly skilled workforce that has the ability to adapt to constant change. The sheer complexity of today's businesses and the need for specialized skills demand that organizations take a quantitative approach to optimizing workforce training investments and human resource allocation. Fortunately, the knowledge is emerging to navigate and even leverage this complexity. Predictive analytics, a quantitative approach to unveiling and measuring patterns from large amounts of data, has the ability to extract and quantify patterns and relationships that can be used to guide human capital decisions. A thoughtful blend of predictive analytics, good problem-solving skills, and common sense go a long way to developing prescriptions for effective human capital investments, as well as human resource actions and interventions.

—Olivia Parr-Rud, OLIVIA Group

Ignoring human capital analytics in the hopes that it's a passing fad puts you at risk of becoming obsolete. The forces behind it are too powerful. First, there is supply; technology advances have made HR data available on a scale that was heretofore unimaginable. But more important is demand. The growing economic premium associated with superior human capital management means that HR strategy is simply too important to be left to intuition. The only question is whether HR will step up to the plate or whether finance will do the job for HR.

—Laurie Bassi, McBassi & Co.

FINAL THOUGHTS

The value proposition an enterprise has created has shifted. The value of a modern company is in the intangibles, most of which are human capital of one form or another: expertise, customer relationships, employer brand, intellectual property, business concepts. The market has recognized this; in the 1980s, 85 percent of the value of a company was in tangibles such as brick and mortar, and now it has shifted to the opposite, with 85 percent of the value being in the intangibles.[2] The data space describing our enterprises has shifted as well. There has been an explosion in the quantity of data available and the computational power we have to exploit it. What are you going to do about these changes? The only real option is to work smarter, not harder. The companies that will thrive and prosper are those that get the most out of their human capital, and that requires you to understand what is going on with your workforce and how your investments affect it and to communicate those changes effectively with all parts of the enterprise.

We hope this book has put some useful tools in your hands and inspired you with the will and enthusiasm to use them. Good luck, and good hunting.

NOTES

1. J. W. Boudreau, *Retooling HR: Using Proven Business Tools to Make Better Decisions about Talent* (Boston: Harvard Business School, 2010).
2. M. E. Echols, *ROI on Human Capital Investment* (Wyomissing, PA: Tapestry Press, 2005).

Appendix A

Different Levels to Describe Measurement

The more you know about how the pieces of a project can be classified or viewed from different angles, the easier it is to be creative with finding new metrics, new demographic descriptors, and more innovative ways of viewing your company's business processes. You can be more confident that you have considered your options and chosen the best set for a given project. In this appendix, we will show you the basic math building blocks and also delve into several different scales that are widely used within learning and development: Kirkpatrick/ Phillips, Bersin, and Spitzer. We will also cover the Six Boxes Model, which is about performance improvement but is so useful that we feel compelled to include it.

Let's start at the beginning, with mathematics. Math has a basic set of descriptors about how to measure things. It divides variables into four types:

1. *Nominal* variables are those that separate data into categories but do not have a numerical value associated with them. Variables you might come across in human capital are the demographic descriptors, such as region, gender, or race. Nominal is sometimes called categorical.

2. *Ordinal* variables are those measured with a number that indicates placement relative to other items, but the placement does not specify some exact quantity. For example, if I finish fourth in a race, I am not half as fast as the number-two finisher or twice as fast as the number-eight finisher. "Fourth" might be

171

split seconds or hours away from those two values, and I know nothing about the time for the first-place finisher. When a survey respondent is asked to rate something, such as his or her satisfaction with the service, on a numerical scale, this is a commonly encountered example of ordinal data. Scales of this type are called "Likert scales."

3. *Interval* data is a type of data where the numbers have more meaningful gaps between them than ordinal data does, but where the starting point is arbitrary. The Fahrenheit temperature scale is an example. The 10-degree difference between 30 and 40 degrees has exactly the same meaning as that between 40 and 50 degrees. The intervals may be meaningfully added and subtracted. However, the starting points and ending points of interval data might not be meaningful: zero degrees in Fahrenheit has no particular reason it is zero, other than a historical footnote about how the scale was originally constructed.

4. *Ratio* data is how most measurement is done in the sciences, where the number has a meaningful starting and ending point, and the intervals between numbers are meaningful. Examples are items that are counted and have a meaningful zero point, monetary data, or weights and distances. If I sold 100 units last month, and you sold 50, I sold twice as much, and you sold twice as much as the person with 25. If I add the sales for the three of us together, we sold 175.

KIRKPATRICK SCALE

The best-known scale in learning and development is the Kirkpatrick scale.[1] It, like our analytics continuum, makes the assumption that measurement complexity and usefulness increase as you go along. Kirkpatrick makes the assumption that a learning and development (L&D) investment was made, however, because a couple of the levels don't make sense except in an L&D context. Kirkpatrick's four levels have been augmented in common usage over the years, and we identify six levels here:

Level 0: Usage. Usage is how many people take advantage of a training program. This was not in the original Kirkpatrick scale (as you might guess by the numbering), and it became recently popular among the learning management systems (LMS) community. Usage is, of course, more of a question when students select courses without instructor intervention. Level 0 measures might include total completions or enrollments.

Level 1: Satisfaction. Satisfaction is the perceived quality of the course by the students. It is usually measured via survey post-training, which are usually referred to as "smile sheets."

Level 2: Learning. Learning is how much of the course content was absorbed by the trainee. It is measured by some sort of test, post-training. To be thorough, a pre-test should also be given, so that the difference can be calculated, although it almost never is.

Level 3: Transfer. Do trainees actually do their jobs differently or "transfer" the new learned behaviors to the workplace? Transfer is measured by direct observation, preferably, or by surveys. One common practice we see in customer service is to use the consumer as a check on transfer (e.g., "Get a free meal if you are not given a receipt").

Level 4: Business impact. This is our favorite, of course. What is the change in key performance indicators caused by the training program? This book is largely about level 4, so we will not discuss it much here.

Level 5: Return on investment. This important addition was added by Jack Phillips.[2] Phillips has been spokesperson for ROI, and his contribution has been huge. The extra math and effort added to go to level 5 is not profound, but the change in focus is. Level 5 circles us back to the idea of *business* impact. If the training does not make money, why are we doing it?

The Kirkpatrick levels engender some disagreement as to exactly what fits into what level. We have heard the phrase "Kirkpatrick model" being used to describe a process of measuring at some or all of the five levels, which is not really a correct usage; Kirkpatrick is a taxonomy, not a process. Others have proposed a "Kirkpatrick Plus" framework that adds "Societal impact" as an additional level, rather than the Phillips ROI.[3] Others have added a sixth level of "Sustainability" and a seventh level of "Sharing the benefit."[4] We have often used the phrase "level 6" ourselves to describe optimization.

There are other scales that are less well known but show some usefulness.

THE SPITZER LEARNING EFFECTIVENESS MODEL

The Spitzer Learning Effectiveness Model (LEM) is a different take on measurement and evaluation, because it tries to take the focus away from a post-hoc "measurement and evaluation"—the levels are based on *when* you measure. The idea is to start at the beginning of the process and work through, point by point, to show the desired changes in business, building causal chains. The five levels are:

1. **Predictive measurement** is what *should* happen as the result of the investment. This is what we call alignment or, from an L&D perspective, a skill-gap analysis.

2. **Baseline measurement** is done before the implementation of the investment, to identify the current state and help estimate target values.

3. **Formative measurement** is done during the intervention design to make sure the data are available for the design and implementation plan.

4. **In-process measurement** is done during implementation to track investment during deployment and allow timely corrections.

5. **Retrospective measurement** is done after the investment is complete to provide input for future decision making.

Spitzer's LEM involves a detailed analysis process and development of an understanding of the business need, beyond a traditional training needs analysis process. Measurement is done not only afterward, but before and during the training process. This identification of the business issues and causal chain up front also leads to major changes in the way learning interventions are designed. Oftentimes, traditional training programs are bypassed in favor of on-the-job mentoring programs and job aids that are viewed as a short-cut to the desired outcomes.

THE BERSIN MODEL

Josh Bersin has been regarded as a learning leader and influential speaker, author, and consultant for many years, and Bersin & Associates has been a major source for learning and HR decision makers since 2001. The organization provides a wide and holistic perspective on analyzing corporate investments; its High-Impact Measurement Framework uses nine driving forces:

1. Satisfaction

2. Learning

3. Adoption

4. Utility

5. Efficiency

6. Alignment

7. Attainment of customer objectives

8. Individual performance

9. Organizational performance

The framework is wide enough to take into account the Kirkpatrick and Phillips hierarchies, as well as the Brinkerhoff success-case methodology.

THE SIX BOXES MODEL

The Six Boxes model is not a measurement and evaluation framework but a categorization of the basic factors that affect human behavior in the workplace, called *behavior influences*. The model allows users to identify existing behavior influences—those that enable and those that obstruct desired behavior—and is commonly used for needs analysis, program design, implementation planning, and change management, among other applications. The top row of Exhibit A.1 describes

Exhibit A.1 The Six Boxes Model of Behavior Influence
Source: Used by permission of the Performance Thinking Network

organization factors, and the bottom row describes individual performer factors. The Six Boxes model was developed by Carl Binder, who adopted plain English for rapid learning and communicating concepts derived from Thomas Gilbert's original work on the behavioral engineering model.[5]

Note that training is only one way to provide skills and knowledge, the behavior influence represented in box 4 of Exhibit A.1.[6] The Six Boxes model is to help practitioners remember that training is only one of many solutions to a performance problem and that it is seldom sufficient by itself.

THE HCM:21 MODEL

Predictive analytics rides on two factors: logical questioning and mathematical analysis. People often start an analytic project by asking, "What should we measure?" This should be the last question that is asked. Jac Fitz-Enz's model of HCM:21 (Human capital management for the twenty-first century) contains four sections:[7]

1. Scanning
2. Planning

3. Process optimization
4. Prediction

Scanning

In order to manage tomorrow we need to know to the best of our ability what the future will look like. The best way to learn that is to ask ourselves what relevant variables are likely to impact the management of our human capital. We obtain this knowledge through what we call situational assessment. This is a matrix that consists of the three forms of organizational capital: human, structural, and relational. Human capital are the employees. Structural capital are the things the organization owns. Relational capital are typically outside stakeholders, such as customers, suppliers, competitors, regulators, and the communities in which an organization does business. For these three aspects, both external and internal factors need to be considered. External forces are the economy, labor pool, technology, competition, and globalization. Internal forces are leadership, readiness, finances, capabilities, and brand.

We need to know how these variables will interact to affect human capital management in the future. Without this knowledge we are flying blind. Conversely, with this foundation we can begin workforce planning and improvement programs.

Planning

Planning is risk management. Projections are never 100 percent correct and seldom work out as expected. Essentially, twenty-first-century planning is about developing the human capabilities needed for success in tomorrow's market. We can do this if we ask ourselves how current competencies must evolve into future capabilities. Again, we need to examine how technology, customers, competition, and so on will drive change in our employee base. A new force to be reckoned with is social networking and its effects on employee connectivity, values, and expectations.

Process Optimization

After planning we must act by examining our human resource delivery systems. What are we delivering and in what manner? Analytics help us find the most cost-effective way to hire, pay, develop, and retain talent. For example, in the recruitment and selection process, where are the most effective sources of applicants and what are the most effective screening and on-boarding methods to obtain employees who perform well, have growth potential, and stay with the organization? Statistical analysis can help answer that.

Prediction

Most data that organizations collect focus on the past (i.e., lagging indicators). Sales, expenses, productivity, and service level data are records of past performance, which are no longer manageable. We need to collect data on leading indicators. Chief among these are leadership, engagement, readiness, culture, and retention. Each of these has the capacity to give us clues as to the future of our organization. Again, statistical analysis can yield insights as to the future state of our workforce and, therefore, our odds of success.

SUMMARY

The axiom that past is prologue is not nearly as true as it used to be. Tomorrow is looking less and less like yesterday. The markets and, indeed, the twenty-first-century world are increasingly unstable and unpredictable. We need to apply all available resources in order to survive and succeed in this new world. Chief among these is predictive analytics.

NOTES

1. D. L. Kirkpatrick, "Evaluating Training Programs: Evidence vs. Proof," *Training & Development Journal* 31, no. 11 (1977): 9–12.
2. J. J. Phillips, *Return on Investment in Training and Performance Improvement Programs* (Houston: Gulf Publishing Company, 1997).

APPENDIX A ◀ 179

3. R. Watkins, D. Leigh, R. Foshay, and R. Kaufman, "Kirkpatrick Plus: Evaluation and Continuous Improvement with a Community Focus," *Educational Technology Research and Development* 46, no. 4 (1998): 90–96.

4. A. Rylatt, *Winning the Knowledge Game: Smarter Learning for Business Excellence* (London: Butterworth-Heineman, 2003).

5. T. F. Gilbert, *Human Competence: Engineering Worthy Performance, Washington, DC: International Society for Performance Improvement,* 1978; republished in 1996; C Binder, "The Six Boxes: A Descendent of Gilbert's Behavior Engineering Model," *Performance Improvement.* 37, no. 6 (1998): 48–52.

6. C. Binder, "What's So New About the Six Boxes® Model?" http://www.sixboxes.com/_customelements/uploadedResources/160039_SixBoxesWhatsSoNew.pdf, accessed July 10, 2012.

7. J. Fitz-Enz, *The New HR Analytics: Predicting the Economic Value of Your Company's Human Capital Investments* (New York: Amacom, 2010).

Appendix B

Getting Your Feet Wet in Data: Preparing and Cleaning the Data Set

The purpose of this book is to provide a road map for pursuing and executing an analytic approach to human capital investment. It is written at the 10,000-foot level so as to cover a broad range of scenarios. However, if you are looking for practical tips and specific techniques for analyzing the data, this appendix is for you.

You will never be able to find out whether your intervention is having the desired effect if your data aren't fully cleaned and prepped prior to statistical analysis. Depending on the complexity of your data and your project, this can be one of the more time- and resource-consuming aspects of the project. Engaging the data analyst who will be working on your project when the study is designed can be a big time saver. He or she can help you work with your data owners to develop the data requirements for the project, ensuring that all needed columns are included and determining the most efficient format for the exported data. Having to go back to a data owner to ask for additional data can have a huge impact on the project time line.

DATA PRIVACY AND ENCRYPTION

Data privacy is increasingly becoming an important concern for many organizations. With more connectivity and electronic access, it is critical to protect personal information. One very useful technique is the removal of personally identifying information. This involves stripping the employee records down to a record ID or employee number and allows you to remove the proper name, the address, and so on. If further privacy is desired, some algorithm can be used to mask the identifier by changing into a different form in a way that allows it to be done across several different databases. "Hashing techniques" map information to a simple code or number in a unique, repeatable way; your IT staff can help you with these. Even if the original data could be recovered eventually, it at least adds an extra layer of protection from prying eyes.

Discuss with your IT professional or systems administrator what security mechanisms are protecting your data and whether more are needed. Strong passwords, encryption, and ensuring the physical safety of the computer holding the data are all concepts you should discuss. If the data leave the building, take appropriate precautions (your IT colleague can help you identify these). Sending data in unencrypted e-mail (or, which is somewhat baffling, encrypting the data and sending the password along with it in plain text) is a bad idea. Remember, the data sets you will be developing offer powerful insights into your company's performance, and the information is all the more important to protect.

GETTING YOUR FEET WET IN THE DATA

Once you have secured data for your project, you should begin working with the data as soon as possible. Learn as much as you can early on. As explained in the discussion in Chapter 3 on analytics personnel, a data analyst is a key position in a measurement project and is the first point of entry for the data into your analytics team. The format of the data you request should be somewhat determined by the skill sets of the staff you have available. For example, spreadsheets are the most common, but more complex databases can be useful if you have the skill sets to take advantage of such formats. The most general, widely readable format is the CSV (comma separated variable) text file that can be imported into almost any tool.

What Tools to Use

Unless you are working with very large datasets, a lot of the data preparation can be done in Microsoft Excel or Open Office Calc.

However, larger projects—those with a greater number of rows or columns of data or having many different sources of data—often require the use of more advanced tools such as relational databases like Microsoft SQL Server, MySQL, or Oracle.

Statistical analysis is typically best suited to statistical packages such as SAS, SPSS, or R (a free, open-source tool), but Excel can be used for descriptive statistics and some basic statistical analyses. Caution should be taken, however, in equating the ability to run a statistical function in Excel with the statistical knowledge needed to correctly craft the question and interpret the output.

The Data Log

We strongly suggest that you keep a project log, with file names, locations, date received, person who provided the data, and a very brief description of the contents. Include the key fields that can be used to match the files together. Keys are simple unique identifiers that run throughout a data set and match to a field in another data set. Make careful notes about what you have and have not received.

You should always maintain an original data folder so that if problems occur, you can back up to a known accurate and correct version. Change the file status to "read only" on those files so that they are not accidentally edited.

VERIFYING COMPLETENESS

It is critical to review the data for completeness. Here are some suggestions for a typical human capital project:

- Make sure that you have all of the files in the data set that you were expecting and that they contain the information required to proceed with the project plan. If you have stakeholder agreement on the period of time to be covered in your measurement project, check to make sure that the files cover that time span. Don't just check the end points—check whether some data in the middle of the range are missing.

▪ Confirm that all groups in the study population are included (for example, both trained and control groups, or terminated and retained employees, and so on). Check for coverage of any important geographic or business grouping classifications.

▪ Check to see whether the amount of data matches up to your knowledge about the organization (for example, is the number of records about the same as the number of employees?). On the flip side, make sure that the data do not include things you were not looking for—out-of-range dates, people from outside the participant groups, and so forth.

▪ Identify columns of data that were not requested but that are included, to see if they might be useful to the study.

CONFIRMING YOUR DATA QUALITY

Before data cleaning and processing start, it is important to confirm that the data received are of an acceptable level of quality and completeness. The following is a suggested list of data quality checks:

1. Is the list of columns complete?

2. Is the number of rows as expected? Does the last row of data look complete? (A bad file transfer can cut the end off a file, as is sometimes evidenced by an incomplete final record.)

3. Review lists of values for coded fields. Are they clear and in line with expectations? For example, if the specifications state that in the Gender column, Female = 1 and Male = 2, are there any values in the data set other than 1 and 2?

4. Verify the range of values in each appropriate column of data. Do any of the columns have values that do not seem to be appropriately distributed or have extreme outliers? For instance, do most of the sales reps have average sales of $50,000, while one rep's average is $800,000? Look at the date fields to ensure that the time frame of data matches the data requirements established when designing the study. (Don't just look at the endpoints; check that the months/quarters/years in the middle are there as well.)

5. Do any required fields have missing values?

6. Are there any duplicate records? You may have to confirm with the data owner whether these are true duplicates or whether some excluded column of data would distinguish them (such that they ought to be retained for the study).

CLEANING UP THE DATA

The degree to which the data will need to be changed from the source will depend on the individual file. The data analyst should consult with the statistician to determine the best format for the files to be analyzed. Different statistical packages have different requirements as to format, column headings, and so on. A mix of lower- and upper-case in column values, such having "M," "m," "F," and "f" as codes for "Male" and "Female," may be read as two different values by some systems and as four by others.

If you are cleaning the data in Excel, specifying the data types of the columns can help uncover inconsistencies in the values received. Turning on Filtering is a quick way to look at the list of unique values present in a column of data (and can help you find unexpected values or misspellings/miscodings).

If you must recode any of your columns for the statistician (for instance, if a categorical variable needs to be represented as a number for the analysis), it is a good idea to add a column with the recoded values, rather than replacing the original data. Otherwise, it can be hard to detect an error (and may require starting over from a source data file to correct it).

Dates

Dates can be a major problem area because different systems have different conventions: separating numbers with a slash vs. a dash, whether or not leading zeros appear before single-digit values, and whether years are shown with two digits or four. Similarly, different countries format dates differently, with Americans favoring a mm/dd/yy structure, and Europeans tending to use dd/mm/yy.

When data are transferred between systems, sometimes these different formats lead to an obvious error; other times, the data may appear to load correctly but may actually contain errors. In a past project, one system represented a date as "mm/yy." The next system read those values as "dd/mm" and assumed that the date was for the current year. It was detected only when a sharp-eyed analyst noticed that there was never any data for November or December (the data set ended in 2010, so the last two digits were at most "10").

Graphing the number of data points that occur in each time period (say, month, quarter, or year) can help you discover places where you might be missing data.

Dealing with Outliers

Sometimes, the values of a particular metric are all very similar; in other cases, they may vary dramatically. The decision of whether to include all data points or exclude some as "outliers" can be a difficult choice that can have an impact on the results of the analysis.

COMBINING MULTIPLE DATA SOURCES

It is common to receive project data from multiple sources—for instance, HR (the usual source for demographic and employment information) often uses a different database than the training department or sales. Combining multiple data sources can be a tricky business. Before you start, it is important to ensure that the data received from the different sources is complete and compatible.

1. Verify keys
   a. Are they unique where expected?
   b. Are they consistent across data sources?
   c. In cases of a compound key (e.g., identifying an employee requires knowing both an employee ID and a company code), are all of the necessary columns present in each file?
2. Verify match levels—do records match up as expected? For example, do all of the employees have employment history records?
3. Compare lists of values for fields that are drawn from multiple data sources. Do they match? For example, does each data

source use the same specifications for region? If not, you will need a conversion key from your contacts for each data source.

You might manually line up columns in Excel or use some of its built-in functions, such as vlookup() and hlookup(), when dealing with smaller data sets, but more typically, you will be using some statistical language or database tool.

Once you have combined your files as appropriate, it is a good idea to choose a subset of your data (perhaps a dozen rows) and manually compare the data in your combined file with the source data to ensure that the merge occurred accurately. Whether you are doing this "by hand" or via code you have written, it is easy to make an error that would not be detected without a manual check.

LOOKING FOR PROBLEMS, AND SUGGESTIONS FOR DEALING WITH COMMON ONES

The following are some practical tips on working with data that will smooth the process of conducting a measurement project.

The Sniff Test

The overall point of the exploration of the data is to ensure that it passes the sniff test. Do the data make sense? Is it reasonable and complete? Some discipline in approaching this problem is essential. With a hundred data points, you might look at a dozen in detail, and problems would likely become apparent. With thousands of points, most people feel overwhelmed and don't look at any data, even when looking at that same dozen would have alerted them to problems in the dataset.

Naming Conventions for the Data

It is important in projects of even moderate complexity to develop a standard naming convention for data. Identifying the version of the data, with appropriate filters, inclusions, and exclusions, and being able to identify the columns of the data, will make the project go much smoother. The exact conventions are not particularly important, but having them set up from the beginning will help facilitate the project.

Dealing with Missing Data

Few projects proceed smoothly from start to finish. Even with the vast amounts of data organizations collect today, it is not uncommon to find that the information you need does not exist. Or, if it does exist, it is not in the form you need it. Some hypotheses will turn out to be untenable, and some need to be modified. Here are some of the bumps in the road that might occur. There is no master theory that can enumerate the possible problems and solutions (at least, not yet), but here are some common problems that occur in human capital projects.

The Data Exist But Are at the Wrong Level of Granularity

Suppose you are keen to measure the impact of a new tool that improves the performance of auto mechanics working at service centers. The tool is designed to reduce service times. The first and most central hypothesis is that mechanics who were using the new tool would record quicker service. When the data collection effort begins, a major snag appears: Service times are only tracked on the service center level, and it is not possible to say much about the performance of the individual mechanic. Or is it?

We have done projects like this, and salvaging the project is a matter of redefining the participant. The new hypothesis is: Service centers that provided at least one of the new tools to mechanics will show lower service times.

The information is somewhat less precise and focused but can still provide a very good answer to the ultimate question of evaluating the new tools. Note that this question could be tweaked in several ways— you might ask about "service centers that gave every mechanic the new tool" or "service centers that gave at least half the mechanics a new tool."

Operational Data Couldn't Be Obtained from Certain Sources

One common way around a lack of operational data is to make up for it with survey data. We prefer operational data, of course, but it is better to have some data for decision making than none at all. Don't give up too easily on operational data, because it is closest to the lifeblood of the company! Consider whether there are some alternatives to the data you are looking for that might work. If you don't have data directly on operations, might operations be tracked in other ways? For example, is there a purchase order system or credit card receipts? Is there some sort of compensation based on performance that might mirror the information you need? In one project, we were unable to track the performance of pharmaceutical reps, but we were able to get even more useful data from their customers (physicians).

Data Couldn't Be Matched Up between Sources

Sometimes data are recorded by employee ID; sometimes by e-mail address; sometimes by proper name. Do your different data sources all use the same "primary key"? If so, that's great; you can proceed with the project. If not, consider whether there may be a data set that links together the data you need. Exhibit B.1 shows an example

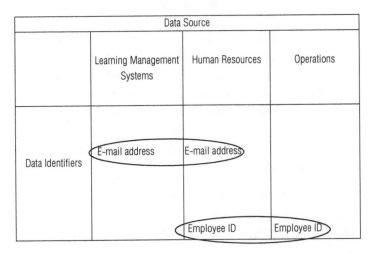

Exhibit B.1 Data Sources

that links operations data and LMS data with human resources data, which has a "map" for the linkage.

A very common problem when merging databases is that a common field has a slightly different name (e.g., "EmpID" vs. "EID" vs. "Employee ID"). Another problem that occurs frequently is minor variations in the keys that link up sources, such as a hyphen as a separator in one data set, where there is a space in the other or a different prefix or suffix, or some other minor and easily fixed issue. A good data analyst has techniques for cleaning these fields. There are software solutions that merge multiple databases together based on "fuzzy matches" that involve multiple fields of data. Yet these are, as of this writing, complex and expensive solutions that are appropriate for databases that manage mailing lists but are not likely feasible for analytics projects.

TRANSFORMING ONE VARIABLE INTO ANOTHER

Alchemy (n): A form of chemistry and speculative philosophy practiced in the Middle Ages and the Renaissance and concerned principally with discovering methods for transmuting baser metals into gold.

■   ■   ■

Suppose you wanted to measure sales or perhaps evaluate whether a sales training program worked. Sales revenue is one metric, right? Not at all—there are many specific metrics involved, not one. Usually, a number of different views or transformations of the data can be more sensitive indicators, can eliminate bias or selection patterns, or can help get you better or, at least, different views of your organization. Taking the example of sales measurement, here are some of the specific measurements that can be used.

- The raw amount of a sale in dollars.
- The number of items sold.
- The number of customers to whom sales were made.
- The average size of a sale.
- Weekly sales.

- Monthly sales.
- The profit margin on a sale.
- Repeat sales.
- Sales of the base item in units.
- Sales of accessories in dollars.
- Percentage of improvement from the same period last year.

For almost any variable, you can create variants based on units, financial values, and percentage increases. We'll go into detail on some of these.

Difference Variables

A very useful variation of a metric is what we call a *difference variable*. A difference variable is created by comparing the value of a participant's data before and after a given date or occurrence. In effect, it measures the change over a given period of time. An example might be to subtract average monthly customer satisfaction ratings taken before a training program from those taken after the program. The main advantage of using the difference score is that it helps control for selection bias for the test and control groups. Another advantage is that it helps reduce the impact of wide variation among participants. A third advantage is that difference variables may be the simplest and most intuitive way to express what is going on with your business processes. For participants in the control group, who do not receive the investment, the before and after dividing point is the median date on which the test group received the investment. Creating a difference variable is a great way to simplify your analysis and control for selection bias. The impact of the investment is calculated by subtracting the difference score for the control group from the difference score for the test group. The only downside of a difference variable is that it can be difficult to quickly get the technique across to an audience.

Percentage Scaled Variables

There are occasions on which it is useful to compare multiple sets of data. For example, if training in your call center decreases average call-handling time by 20 seconds, increases sales by 1.2 units per person per month, and increases retention by 1 extra employee retained per month, what are the relative improvements there? Where is the greatest impact achieved? A solution is to express each of these values as a percentage change from the status quo. When percentage changes are used, improvements can be easily compared. Of course, speaking in the language of the stakeholders is important, so you may wish to socialize preliminary results with them to make sure you are not confusing anyone with a different measurement scale.

Hint: Most people find it most natural to see an improvement as an increase. It is also difficult to mix positive improvements with negative improvements conceptually. For example, sales revenue is supposed to go up, which is a positive improvement, but call-handling time should go down, a negative improvement. When presenting your results, try to use positive improvements, and try to avoid mixing positive and negative improvements. Transformations can be helpful on this. For example, if you wish to change "Average handling time" to "Seconds saved per call," you have turned a negative impact into a positive impact. Please note that we are not suggesting sugar-coating your results in any way, just advising you of ways to provide cognitive shortcuts to help your busy audience understand the results quicker.

Currency Value Variables

One of the ultimate goals of a measurement and evaluation project is to measure the financial impact on the organization. Why not turn your widgets into dollars before beginning the statistical analysis? This can be a better way to communicate with your stakeholders. If several metrics are competing for the attention of the stakeholders, it is good to get a feel for what is important to them. For example, one good way to express the results might be to turn them into currency. (If the analysis includes more than a single country, you may need to convert everything into a single common currency for clarity.) Other stakeholders think almost exclusively in terms of other units, such as failure rate on an assembly line or new vehicles sold.

Appendix C

Details of Basic Descriptive Statistics

Now that you have your data, the first step is to really understand what the data are telling you. Certain important statistical measures can give you a good picture of your underlying data.

Descriptive Statistics

- *Mean*, also called the average, is the sum of values divided through by the number of items.

- *Median*, when values are arranged from highest to lowest, is the one in the middle, or at the fiftieth percentile. Medians, although less familiar of a concept than the mean, are usually more useful, especially if you are trying to get some sense of what is "typical." For example, consider income. If a country has a very small number of super-wealthy individuals, the median value of income may give you a sense of what the typical person is like. If you have 100 people on an island, and they have a "typical" income, the median income might be $50,000. If Bill Gates were to come ashore on that island, the average income would jump to half a billion dollars, though the median would hardly change at all.

- *Mode* is the most commonly scored value in a set. This one is sometimes useful to represent a typical value.

- *Maximum* is the highest value that occurs in a set.

- *Minimum* is the lowest value that occurs in a set.

The idea of variation is also important. In sports, there is the player who is viewed as extremely solid and reliable and usually scores somewhere close to his average. Contrast that with the player who explodes on occasion and then "slumps" or "disappears" in other games. The two players might have the same average, but the coach, sportscasters, and fans will all use a separate vocabulary and separate strategies for this player. The distribution, as previously noted, also gives a lot of feeling to what's going on in the data. Known as measures of "central tendency," there are several ways to measure how tightly the values are clustered around the center. Scatterplots and histograms are good ways to visualize variation. Of the statistics that measure variation, the best known is standard deviation. Please refer to the Glossary for a full description of the calculation.

One of the most common distinctions we make in the data is between continuous and categorical variables. A continuous variable is a number that falls into a range and may vary a lot: salaries, number of units sold, commissions, ages. A categorical variable is one that falls into a fixed number of items: gender, region, whether a performance plan has been filed. There may be some variables, such as customer satisfaction with a 1−5 scale, that can be treated either as categorical or continuous, but that decision is usually left to a statistician.

For continuous variables, such as sales revenue, look for the basic statistics, such as minimum, maximum, average, and median values. Do they make sense? Do you see unrealistic ranges (such as a sales quota of 30 cents or negative values for customer satisfaction)? Sometimes data problems, naming errors, and other factors will produce extremely dysfunctional data. The best thing to do with continuous data is to graph it out. A histogram, illustrated in Exhibit C.1, is a kind of graph that groups values into ranges and represents the number of occurrences of data points within those ranges.

VIEWING THE DATA

Simple graphs are a great way to get a feel for your data, in terms of distribution and completeness.

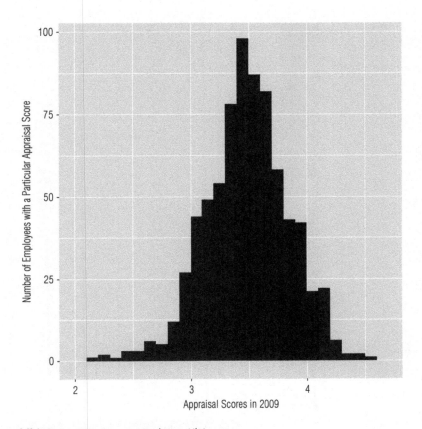

Exhibit C.1 Data Represented as a Histogram

As shown in Exhibit C.1, this data set contains employee appraisal scores for a company, on a 0–5 point score, which can be measured to 2 decimal places (e.g., 4.00 or 3.75 are possible scores). The histogram lumps data points to the nearest tenth of a point. The height of the bar is the number of employees scoring in that range.

Histograms are great ways to look at data, because they can help you spot many different things. At a glance, you can see the maximum and minimum of the range and how the data is distributed. Exhibit D.1 shows what is called a "bell-shaped curve" or a "normal distribution" and is very common in practice. Notice that the center of the graph

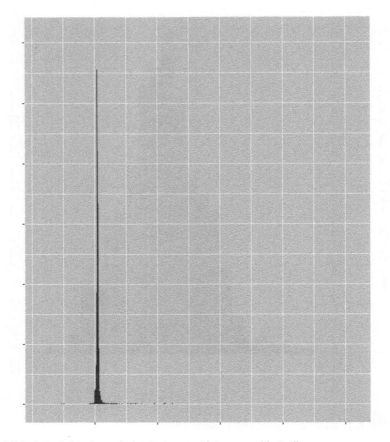

Exhibit C.2   Sales Commission Data as a Histogram with Outliers

shows the biggest concentration of participants, with relatively small outliers. It is found in many natural data sets: think for a minute how many men you know who are between 5½ and 6½ feet, compared to shorter or taller. Most people tend to cluster near an average.

For example, the following pair of graphs (see Exhibits C.2 and C.3) is for sales commission data. The x-axis measures sales commissions, and the height of the bar represents agents who fall into a particular range (e.g., between $900,000 and $1,000,000). Exhibit C.2

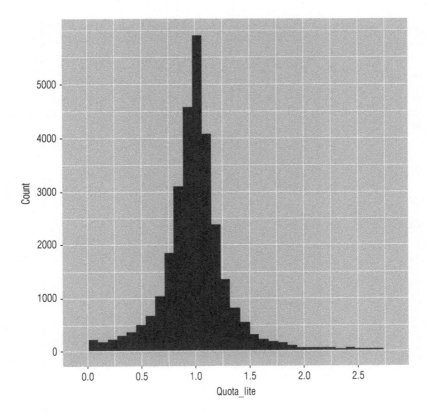

Exhibit C.3 Sales Commission Data as a Histogram with Outliers Removed

is the original data set. A handful of extreme values (outliers) force most of the data to be heavily compressed in the center, making it difficult to see any real distribution. However, when the outliers are removed in Exhibit C.3, we get a much better view of the distribution of most of the data.

Appendix D

Regression Modeling

Regression models quantify the relationship between two variables. Later, we'll talk about how multiple variables can get involved and how variables that are "categorical" can be used, but all of those more complex concepts are just extensions of the basics. Exhibit D.1 shows a small data set taken from a performance improvement system, where the employees were rated on a yearly scale. The question is whether the 2008 ratings correlated strongly with the 2009 ratings—in other words, whether high-performing employees continued to perform highly. The following graph shows the two year's reviews graphed against each other. The pattern seems clear; higher scores in the previous year shows a tendency toward higher scores the next year.

The line that goes through the points looks about right, but how did it get there? The goal of a regression is to minimize the average distance between the line and the points scattered around it. For any regression model, there is exactly one best answer. The equation used in this example is on the chart:

$$y = 0.65314x + 1.16$$

What, exactly, does that mean? The x-axis is last year's rating, and the y-axis is this year's rating. You could write this out as

$$\text{This year} = 0.65314\text{Last year} + 1.16$$

In English, you could say, "For each point you got last year, you get 0.65314 points this year." That number is also known as the slope of the line, or the change in y, given a unit change in x. Another way to

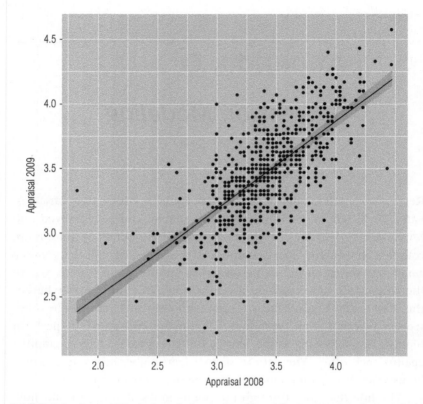

Exhibit D.1 Current Year's Appraisals as a Function of the Previous Year's Appraisals

describe it is the beta-coefficient, a rather technical name, but one that you do see from time to time. What's the 1.16, though? That's called the "intercept," or where the line should cross the y-axis. This might mean that for people who got a 0 rating last year, on average they might get 1.16 points this year (in, I suppose, the same sort of way some tests give you points just for signing your name). There are some cases where the intercept has an intuitive meaning and other cases where it does not. In this case, because there's no one who got a 0 last year, that part of the graph does not mean anything. The beta-coefficient, or slope, is the best estimator you get for the impact of an extra point on last year's evaluation, but variations in the data mean that it is hard to take it literally.

STATISTICAL SIGNIFICANCE

There are a couple of different factors that can go into these tests of statistical significance. The end result is a statistical model. Most of our models can be expressed like this:

Outcome variable = Function of (one or more input variables)

Thus, the previous example might be expressed as:

Number of improved performances
    = Function of (whether they received the investment or not)

In other words, does "whether the person received the investment or not" help us predict whether he or she will do better? Of course, any number of factors might go into our assessment of whether the person might be expected to improve. Perhaps we are talking about sales performance, and we know that those with higher salary bases are maxed out in their performance, so we should account for that factor. Perhaps there are four regions of the country where we have data, and we need to take that into account. Note that there is always a single outcome variable, or key performance indicator, on the left side of the equals sign. There may be any number of factors on the right. Notice that some of these factors, such as training status or gender, are categorical. Others are continuous and might vary over a range, such as salary and tenure within the organization.

We often talk about "statistical significance." It might be the case that there is actually no relationship between the two years of appraisal reports in the previous example. What are the odds that we would see a pattern such as the above if there wasn't a relationship? What if we tried to graph the shoe size of the employee against the appraisal, for example? Statistical significance is the certainty that we are looking at a real pattern and relationship. In the case of Exhibit E.1, the certainty is 99.8 percent. (Software that performs regression analysis will also measure statistical significance.)

What goes into making up statistical significance in a model like this? There are three factors that contribute:

1. **Number of data points**. The more data you have, the better. In the previous example, there are many data points. If we use only a small portion of the data (9 points), the certainty drops to an unacceptable 97 percent. If twice as much data are used, the certainty increases to 99.9 percent.

2. **The effect size**. "Effect size" describes the amount of impact caused by the variable. It is easier to discern the impact of a training program that improves performance by 20 percent than one that improves it by only 2 percent.

3. **Variation of the data**. The regression line is looking for an average (or mean) within the data points. If the data points are fairly consistent and close to the mean, the variation is low. If the data points are spread out away from the average, the variation is much higher. Lower variation leads to higher significance in the model.

In most applications, 95 percent is considered "good enough" as the level of significance, meaning that we are 95 percent certain. However, this means that there is still a 5 percent chance that the relationship is random, so we could be wrong 5 percent of the time. We must ask ourselves, "What is the lowest value that would be acceptable for certainty?" We really don't like going below 95 percent. There are a few cases where we have reported information at around 90 percent, but those are occasions where the prior state of information was really no better than a coin flip. In most of our work, we reach levels of significance that are well over 99 percent.

The R^2 (pronounced "R squared") value (in Exhibit D.2) is often useful in describing the strength of a regression model. R^2 measures how well the model explains the variation in the data, or how tightly the line fits among the points. The R^2 of a model is a percentage that varies between 0 and 1. Exhibit D.2 illustrates the concept. It is best to think of R^2 as one of the more important indicators. When using the same data and objective, a model with a higher R^2 is superior to one with a lower R^2. Other comparisons are not recommended. It is important to note that you can have high statistical significance with a low R^2. In our example, we can say, "We are 99.8 percent confident that 44.64 percent (R-squared) of current year's appraisals can be explained by the previous year's appraisals."

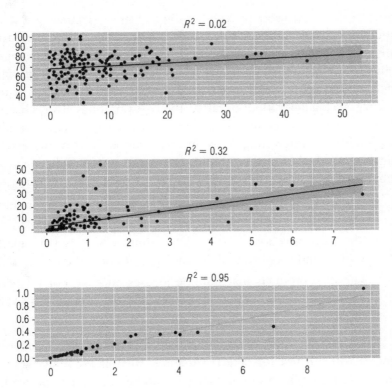

Exhibit D.2 Example of Regressions with Different Values of R^2

REGRESSIONS WITH MORE THAN ONE VARIABLE AND GENERAL LINEAR MODELS

What's the main difference between a regression with two variables and one with three? The previous example is easy to visualize because they can go onto a single graph. When you go to higher numbers of variables, you lose this advantage. The regressions really are much the same, however. You have a statistical significance and an R^2 for the overall model. Each independent variable has its own beta-coefficient and statistical significance, although it does not have an individual R^2.

General linear models are a more powerful model than regressions but have a lot of the same characteristics, yet with one important exception: they can also be used for categorical variables, not only for continuous ones. The data and your imagination are the limit. Other variables, such as region, or whether the person was trained, are some other interesting variables to explore. Interactions take the idea of categorical variables to a new level. The idea is that variables may combine, or interact, in particular ways. Perhaps your sales training is effective and causes sales to go up. Perhaps, also, the region of the country is a big determiner of sales—the East Coast has always been a bigger market, for example. "Interaction" is the idea that two variables can combine in interesting ways. In this example, you would expect that you could add together training status and region and get a good estimate of sales. That isn't always the case. Consider these scenarios:

- The East Coast market is maxed out, and even the great training can't improve sales any more.

- The trainers you were using in the Southwest were particularly skilled, and training gives a much bigger boost there.

- The new products that training focuses on have not yet been approved for the California market, and the training isn't very useful.

These are the kinds of scenarios that interactions were meant to handle. You can test (or detect) situations such as the above. Interactions cut to the heart of optimization—finding out where particular investments are most and least effective.

OTHER TYPES OF MODELS

Regression, multivariable regression, and general linear models (GLMs) are some of the most useful techniques we have in our tool-box, but that's not all we use. We also use structural equation modeling (SEM), which is a way of automatically testing a wide variety of possible scenarios with GLM-type tests. Monte Carlo simulation is a way of testing the likelihood of future situations, given some probabilistic knowledge about the current state of the world. Cronbach's alpha helps us tell whether items on a survey or test were strong or weak contributors to the overall conclusions provided. These are only a few of the many, many models out there. There are literally hundreds of kinds of models and tests that have been applied to economics, physics, medical research, and so forth, that have yet to be vetted for human capital work but that show promise.

Appendix E

Generating Soft Data from Employees

Why rely on interviews when data are available? We often rail against the subjective nature of talking to individuals, rather than looking at their behavior and performance, but we do supplement hard data with qualitative sources. Sometimes interviewing is a good way to understand a business process before a more rigorous analysis can be undertaken. There are many possible interventions to get closer to a strategic goal and many different ways of measuring whether a company is getting there. If you are new to a business or are encountering significant disagreement about the goals from your stakeholders, interviewing those who are acknowledged to be successful will help you understand the problem area, identify some interventions that are believed to be useful, and identify KPIs that are important milestones toward the goal.

Not all business processes can be investigated through statistical means. Sometimes, there are few people doing a particular job. An entire branch of computer science called expert systems is designed to construct computer systems around providing expert diagnosis and problem solving in domains where such advice is scarce, expensive, or geographically distant.[1] There are a number of different interviewing techniques. The simplest, where many people often start, is the *unstructured interview*. An unstructured interview is simply a conversation with an expert about the domain of interest.[2] It has the advantage of relatively easy preparation, which often produces serendipitous information. However, it does not always provide complete coverage of the topic area. Participants may not accurately report their real thought processes but instead present a highly structured, cleaned-up version.

A *structured interview* is a goal-oriented, organized dialogue between the interviewer and the person operating in the domain. It allows you to focus on the problems you need to solve, reducing the expert's tendency to go off on tangents. There are a number of different ways to add structure to an interview. One type of structured interview is to collect a series of problems to be diagnosed or solved and ask the subject to guide you through a solution to them. Another type is to prepare checklists of interventions and metrics and ask the subject about the relationships among them, as well as about their relative value. A variant that has been successful is the semistructured interview, where the expert is allowed to work freely on a problem or is asked very general questions. At some point in the interview, the checklist can be used to prompt the subject about issues that have not yet surfaced. This allows the interviewer to be complete, yet lets the subject provide, in a way unbiased by the interviewer, a sense of the most important features and even generate new information to the interviewer. Brinkerhoff has developed a well-thought-out methodology for drilling down into positive results to understand and replicate how those "wins" occurred, called Success Case Methodology.[3]

Interview results can be analyzed in a variety of ways. If the interview consists of quantitative questions (similar to surveys, with Likert scales or multiple choice answers), standard statistical techniques may be appropriate. Generally, however, if you are doing interviews, you are seeking richer, more general information. The most basic idea in interview analysis is that of coding. Coding is basically the idea that certain recurring concepts (such as good customer service or handling a difficult customer) are present in the transcript of an interview and need to be noted, indexed, and catalogued. Methods range from simple techniques, such as marking up a text document with color-coded highlighters or Post-It notes, to computer-aided qualitative data analysis software (CAQDAS), with commercially available software such as Atlas-ti, MAXqda, and Transana.

There are other techniques that apply to specific kinds of situations. Observation is simply watching someone perform his or her job. It is a direct way of measuring transfer (whether learning "transferred"

from the classroom to the job site), looking for efficiency improvements, and learning more about a task. Protocol analysis is a technique
where someone is asked to do some problem solving and verbalize his
or her thoughts while doing it; obviously, it has limited applications. A
common term for an unstructured group problem-solving activity is
brainstorming.

NOTES

1. P. Jackson, *Introduction to Expert Systems* (Boston: Addison-Wesley Longman,
   1990).
2. H. R. Rueter and J. R. Olson, "Psychological Tools for Knowledge Acquisition," *Proceedings of the Second Annual Workship on Space Operations, Auto-
   mation, and Robotics* (SOAR '88), Dayton, Ohio (1988).
3. R. O. Brinkerhoff, *The Success Case Method: Find Out Quickly What's Working
   and What's Not* (San Francisco: Berrett-Koehler, 2003).

Glossary

ANOVA:
A statistical technique that helps in making inference for whether three or more samples might come from populations having the same mean; specifically, whether the differences among the samples might be caused by chance variation. ANOVA is used in situations where a single factor is believed to account for differences in the data, and that factor allows us to lump the observations into a small number of discrete categories.

Business metric:
A continuous variable of interest in a data set. A business metric may be used as a dependent or an independent variable.

Business outcome:
The dependent variable you select in a statistical question. You select a single business outcome from the set of business metrics.

Categorical variable:
A variable whose values are a finite, restricted set of enumerated values. Examples might include *gender* (male or female) or *job title* (engineer, salesman, manager).

Coefficient of determination:
See *R-squared (R^2)*.

Cohort:
A group of people who have a feature in common, particularly being of the same generation or entering a school or a company at the same time.

Continuous variable:
A variable whose values can vary across a broad range. Continuous variables may be either real numbers or integers, or they may fall into a restricted range (such as 0 to 100). Compare with *Categorical variable*.

Correlation:
A mutual relationship of two or more things. The degree to which two or more attributes or measurements on the same group of elements tend to vary together.

Cost-to-benefit ratio:
The cost of an intervention divided by the dollar benefit estimated to accrue to the participants.

Data point:
A data point is an observation recorded about some aspect of the company's performance at a particular point in time. A data point usually combines information from the participant, intervention, and metric worksheets. An example might be "Joe Smith, East Region, $30,200, 10/2001," which means Joe Smith of the East Region sold $30,200 in October 2001.

Dependent variable:
In a statistical question, the value of interest as an outcome. A single dependent variable is said to depend on one or more independent variables.

Effect size:
The amount of change in a dependent variable contributed by a particular change in an independent variable.

Factor:
A factor is a variable that can have different values that you believe affect a business outcome. In statistics, factors are referred to as *independent variables*. Factors might be an intervention, such as training, or any relevant piece of information, such as the region a salesperson operates in, the type of equipment a factory worker uses, or the amount of bonus pay received last year.

Function:
A function is a mathematical formula where one or more input variables produce a single numerical output.

Full model:
In statistical questions, when independent variables are added to a question, it is important to ask how much those independent variables contribute to your understanding of the data. For example, if you

want to know whether training affects sales, you might re-ask the question as:

Does adding the variable "training" to my question tell me more about sales than simply knowing the average sales figures?

To phrase this question in a very mathematical way, does the model:

Sales = Average Sales + Training + Random Variation (Full Model)

tell me more than:

Sales = Average Sales + Random Variation (Reduced Model)?

The full model is the version of the question that contains the independent variable of interest, whereas the reduced model is the one that does not. The F-statistic and the p-value allow us to compare whether the added complexity of the full model really provides us with much better information. If training was really useful, we would expect to be able to better predict a salesperson's performance if we knew whether he or she was trained (which would lead to a higher F-value, and a lower p-value). If training was of no use, the extra variable would not provide a better guess (and, hence, we would get a low value for F and a high value for p).

General linear model:
A statistical test that answers whether a single dependent variable is a function of one or more independent variables. The independent variables may consist of a mixture of continuous and categorical variables.

Granularity:
In a data point for a metric or an intervention, the precision of the time measurement (e.g., monthly, yearly, daily).

Independent variable:
In a statistical question, a factor or a variable, such as training, that affects the value of a dependent variable. For a single dependent variable, there may be multiple independent variables.

Interaction:
Interaction in a statistical model indicates that two or more of the independent variables have a synergy between them. Interaction

requires that the values of both variables be understood. As an example, suppose that the sales figures for all representatives in a sporting goods company were measured. Further assume that two independent variables were also recorded: whether the sales representative had participated in training, and the region of the country. It may be the case that the training had an overall positive effect and also that the different regions of the company sell different amounts on the average.

In the following examples, trained salespeople have an average sales figure, which is $20,000 higher than untrained salespeople, and the Southern region is noticeably higher than other regions.

Condition	Average
Trained	$191,231
Untrained	$171,231

Region	Average
North	$191,231
East	$199,456
West	$197,256
South	$222,789

It may be the case that the regions of the country are not affected in the same way by training. For example, perhaps sales representatives in the South are reaching the limit of how many sales the warehouses in that region are able to ship, and additional training will not improve sales in that region. As another example, suppose that the training focused on some aspect of selling sporting goods that does not apply equally to all regions of the country; perhaps the instructor provided a great deal of information about how to sell hockey or snow-skiing equipment that was of less use to representatives in the South. Another possible scenario might be that the South has a higher concentration of expert sales representatives who have little extra to learn from the training offered. Exhibit 1 illustrates these hypothetical situations. Note that the lines for each of three other regions show a noticeable improvement between "trained" and "untrained," whereas the South shows a relatively flat, unsloped line, indicating little improvement from training.

When such situations occur, they are said to be interactions and may tell you very interesting things about your data.

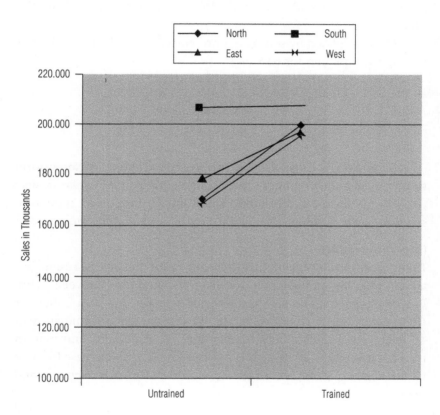

Exhibit 1 Regional Sales by Trained versus Untrained

Intercept:
In an equation, the value on the y-axis that corresponds to $x = 0$.

Internal rate of return (IRR):
The internal rate of return (IRR) method determines the interest rate required to make the present value of the cash flow equal to

zero. It represents the maximum rate of interest that could be paid if all project funds were borrowed and the organization had to break even on the projects. The IRR considers the time value of money and is unaffected by the scale of the project. It can be used to rank alternatives and used to make accept/reject decisions on a project. It assumes returns are invested at the same internal rate of return. It may make alternatives with high rates of return look particularly good and those with low rates of return look particularly bad.

IRR is calculated by setting net present value (NPV) to 0 and back solving the equation for NPV.

For one year, the closed-form solution is:

$$IRR = 100 \times \left(\frac{Gross\ Benefit}{Cost} - 1.0 \right)$$

The answer is calculable for two years and more. A closed-form solution using the quadratic equation is available at two years; a simpler solution is to use a bisection algorithm or some other numerical solution (such as Newton's method) for values 2 and higher.

Interval variables:
These allow us not only to rank order the items that are measured, but also to quantify and compare the sizes of differences between them. For example, temperature, as measured in degrees Fahrenheit or Celsius, constitutes an interval scale. We can say that a temperature of 40 degrees is higher than a temperature of 30 degrees, and that an increase from 20 to 40 degrees is twice as much as an increase from 30 to 40 degrees. Compare to *ratio variable* and also to *nominal* and *ordinal.*

Isolation:
Any technique that allows the effect of an investment to be measured accurately and separated from selection bias and other factors that muddy the water.

Key performance indicator (KPI):
A key performance indicator is an important metric that measures one of your business processes.

Level:
For a categorical variable, a value that it can take on.

Likert scale:
A numerical scale that a survey respondent uses to give a response. For example, "On a 5-point scale, with 1 being the worst, and 5 being the best, how would you rate your customer experience?"

Linear regression:
A statistical technique that describes the relationship between a dependent variable and one or more independent variables. Both the dependent and the independent variables must be continuous numeric values or ordered categorical variables. The technique involves fitting the best line through the set of data points to minimize the difference between their actual distance from the line and their predicted difference from that line. Linear regression produces a parameter estimate that describes how much each unit of an independent variable adds to the value of the dependent variable.

Main effect:
A single independent variable is said to have a *main effect* if the dependent variable shows a clear and reliable trend based on that independent variable. For example, if the independent variable is categorical with levels of true and false, a main effect is said to exist if the average value of the dependent variable for true items differs significantly from that of false items. Main effects may occur without an interaction, and vice versa.

Mean:
The average of a set of data.

Median:
In a set of data, the median is the value below which 50 percent of the values fall; the midpoint. Medians are preferable to averages in data where a few extreme values might skew the average.

Net present value:
A way of quantifying discounted cash flow:

$$NPV = CF_0 + \frac{CF_1}{(1+i)^1} + \frac{CF_2}{(1+i)^2} + \cdots + \frac{CF_n}{(1+i)^n}$$

where CF_i is the cash flow at time t_i, and i is the interest rate.

Net profit margin:
The percentage of net income generated by each dollar of sales. It can be used as retained earnings or is distributed to shareholders as dividends. Compare to *gross profit margin*.

Nominal variables:
A type of variable that allows only qualitative classification. That is, they can be measured only in terms of whether the individual items belong to some distinctively different categories, but we cannot quantify or even rank order those categories. For example, all we can say is that two individuals are different in terms of variable A (e.g., they are of different race), but we cannot say which one "has more" of the quality represented by the variable. Typical examples of nominal variables are gender, race, color, city, type of degree, and so on. We use the phrase *categorical variable* synonymously.

Ordinal variables:
These allow us to rank order the items we measure in terms of which has less and which has more of the quality represented by the variable, but still they do not allow us to say "how much more." A typical example of an ordinal variable is the socioeconomic status of families. For example, we know that upper-middle is higher than middle, but we cannot say that it is, for example, 18 percent higher. Also, this very distinction between nominal, ordinal, and interval scales itself represents a good example of an ordinal variable. For example, we can say that nominal measurement provides less information than ordinal measurement, but we cannot say "how much less" or how this difference compares to the difference between ordinal and interval scales.

p-value:
In a statistical model, the measure of surety for the model. The p-value, formally stated, is the chance that random variation in the data accounts for the patterns seen just, as well as the proposed question. Note that p-values are typical written as

$$p < .05$$

which is read as "the probability that we reached such a conclusion incorrectly is less than 5 percent." This level (5 percent) is regarded as an adequate standard of proof in most situations.

Note that the *p*-value is the inverse of the certainty:

$$C = 1 - P$$

Percentile:
A way of ranking participants on some value. Percentile value gives the percentage of other participants who scored lower than the given participant on that value. For example, if the participant is in the twenty-second percentile, it means that 22 percent of the participants in the data set had a lower value for the metric (and 77 percent of participants had a higher value).

***R*:**
A popular open-source programming language for statistics and graphics. *R* is particularly notable for having hundreds of separate packages written by its user community that cover almost every conceivable analysis technique.

R-squared:
Also called R^2 or the coefficient of determination. Informally, this is a number ranging between 0 and 1 that describes how much of the variation in the dependent variable data is accounted for by the independent variables specified in a statistical model or question. A value of 0 indicates that the independent variables have no influence at all on the data; 1.0 indicates that if the values of the independent variables are known, the value of the dependent variable is known with no error at all. *R*-squared is formally defined as

$$R^2 = \frac{SSR}{SST}$$

where *SSR* is the sum of squares in the full model, and *SST* is the total sum of squares. By the sum of squares, we mean the sum of squared deviations between actual values and the mean (*SST*), or between predicted values and the mean (*SSR*).

Random selection:
A technique for selecting participants in an intervention where any participant in the pool of participants has an equal chance of selection. Methods used to implement random selection might include drawing

the name out of a hat, flipping a coin, or using a computer program designed for random number selection. In contrast to random selection, many corporate training programs select participants based on high or low performance, tenure with the company, geographic location, or other factors. Random selection is always preferable from an experimental design and statistical point of view because prior performance need not be taken into account.

Ratio variables:
Very similar to interval variables; in addition to all of the properties of interval variables, they feature an identifiable absolute zero point, thus, they allow for statements such as x is two times more than y. Typical examples of ratio scales are measures of time or space. For example, as the Kelvin temperature scale is a ratio scale, not only can we say that a temperature of 200 degrees is higher than a temperature of 100 degrees, we can correctly state that it is twice as high. Interval scales do not have the ratio property. Most statistical data analysis procedures do not distinguish between the interval and ratio properties of the measurement scales.

Reduced model:
The opposite of a *full model.*

Return on investment (ROI):
For an investment, the percentage return one receives from it. *ROI* is calculated as:

$$ROI = \frac{Gross\ Benefit - Cost}{Cost}$$

where *Cost* is the cost of training or other intervention, and *Gross Benefit* is the amount of increase seen in a business metric. Unless otherwise specified, the assumption is that cost is incurred a single time, and that benefits are calculated for one full year. If more than a one-year *ROI* calculation is specified, where the *ROI* is requested for n years, the percentage returned is

$$ROI = \frac{1}{n} \sum_{y=1}^{n} \frac{Gross\ Benefit_i - Cost}{Cost}$$

where *Cost* is incurred a single time.

SAS:
A popular statistics analysis package. It is considered the gold standard for statistical analysis but requires significant expertise to program and interpret the results.

Selection bias:
Selection biases are systematic differences that occur in selecting people for an investment. For example, in many companies there is a selection bias that high performers are more likely to be chosen for training. When surveys are used and there is a low return rate, selection bias is a major concern. Note that self-selection bias is just a specific case of a selection bias.

Self-selection bias:
A self-selection bias occurs when people volunteer for some experience, such as training, and those people differ in particular ways from nonvolunteers. For example, we often see that people who seek out training are usually already performing at a higher level.

Significant:
In a statistical model, an independent variable is said to be *significant* if there is a high likelihood that the variable influences the dependent variable. The significance is usually expressed as a percentage, such as "$p < .05$." The number indicates the percentage under which the values seen in the data set might have occurred by pure chance. In the example of $p < .05$, there is a 5 percent chance (1 in 20) of such a likelihood. In most statistics, if something is said to be "significant," it is understood that there is less than a 5 percent chance of the data values producing this result by coincidence. Put another way, a significance of 95 percent means that 95 percent of the time the experiment or event reoccurs, the conclusion would be the same.

Slope:
See the definition of *intercept* for an explanation of slope.

Standard deviation:
A measure of how widely the data points tend to diverge from the mean. A small standard deviation indicates most values are close to the mean, and a large standard deviation indicates they are much more or much less than the mean. The basic idea is that you'd

like to sum up how different the individual data points are from the average. You could just sum up the individual differences, but what about the fact that some are less than the mean and others are greater? That would tend to make them cancel out. The way to get around that is to square the differences, because any time you square a number, the result is positive. Later, after we have added them together, we take a square root, to reduce the value down to something more manageable and reasonable. That's all there is to it. The equation for the standard deviation is:

$$= \sqrt{\frac{1}{n-1} \sum_{i=1}^{n} (x_\mu - x_i)^2}$$

Note that squaring the difference and then taking the square root of the sum cancels out the sign of the difference. The distribution, as previously noted, also gives a lot of feeling to what's going on in the data. There are several ways to measure "central tendency," or how tightly clustered the values are around the center. The best known is standard deviation. The letter sigma (Σ) is used to indicate a set of values added together, and the "mu" (μ) is the standard notation for the "mean."

In most normal distributions, you can take a quick rule of thumb that if you travel 1 standard deviation in each direction from the mean, then that range contains 90 percent of the data. If you go two standard deviations in either direction, 95 percent of the data falls in that range. Three standard deviations in each direction contain 99 percent of the data. There are many cases where this does not work, of course, but it is a good rule to help you generalize.

Statistical paradox:
A case where the data set produces one conclusion when analyzed in a simple way and another conclusion when analyzed in another way. Here's an example. Several years ago, Stanford University decided to analyze whether gender biases existed in its graduate admissions. One set of statistics showed women were rejected at a *much* higher rate than men; another showed that men were rejected at a slightly higher rate than the women. How are both of these conclusions possible? The first set of statistics simply looked at the entire graduate student

application pool and showed that women were rejected at a higher rate. The second set of statistics broke down the applicant pool by school (medicine, law, business, and so on). No single school showed bias; indeed, women were slightly more likely to be admitted than men in some programs. The crucial fact is that women were more likely to apply to the extremely competitive medical and law schools. Thus, although no single department was biased, the distribution of the applicants to the different schools was responsible for the apparent difference.

Trend line analysis:
A technique for presenting and analyzing data. Trend lines typically simplify a graph where different values are shown as dots occurring over time as a scatter plot. Exhibit 2 illustrates daily high temperatures recorded over a month, with the trend line illustrating the average increase. Trend lines are typically a single straight line derived by using linear regression techniques. It is possible to use higher-degree poly-nomials when a more curved line that fits the data more tightly is desired. Trend lines are useful in illustrating overall trends in data. Sometimes trend lines are used to identify and estimate the impact of various events. Although it is a simple technique that does not require a control group or expertise, it cannot definitively separate out the effects of other events.

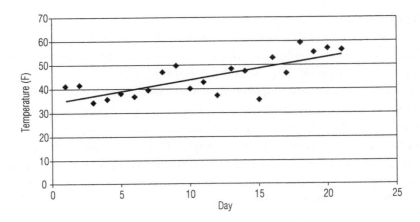

Exhibit 2 High Temperatures Recorded over One Month

Type I error:
This is an incorrect conclusion in which one does not accept a correct hypothesis; for example, if training did benefit participants, and the conclusion was that there were no statistically significant differences between trained and untrained participants. Common causes of type I errors are insufficient sample size, very high variance, or an effect too small to be detected with the sample size and the variances.

Type II error:
This is an incorrect conclusion in which one accepts an incorrect hypothesis; for example, if training did *not* benefit participants, but the report concluded that there was evidence of a benefit. The p-value for a given conclusion represents the chance of a type II error; for example, using $p < 0.05$ implies a 5 percent (1-in-20) chance of a type II error. A hidden and often misunderstood cause of type II errors is a "fishing expedition," wherein a very large set of slightly different post hoc hypotheses or data transformations are used until a desired result is obtained.

Type III error:
This is an incorrect conclusion in which one accepts a logically opposite conclusion from the actual one. For example, suppose that training, for some reason, hurt the performance of the participants. A type III error would be to accept the hypothesis that training benefits the participants. Type III errors are fairly rare.

Type IV error:
Type IV errors indicate that the researcher has correctly accepted the hypothesis that a difference does in fact occur, but he or she has incorrectly assumed that the cell mean differences are the actual differences. For example, suppose that it is known that a given training improves training by 10 percent (assume that 10,000 participants were used, and this is the entire population). Consider a group of only 100 participants who were used as a sample. This group has a 12 percent difference because of sampling error, but the hypothesis that trained and untrained groups differ is confirmed at some level of statistical certainty. Assuming that the actual difference is 12 percent is a type IV

error. An excellent discussion of this poorly understood problem can be found in scientists Joel Levin and Daniel Robinson's article in *Educational Researcher*.[1]

NOTE

1. Joel Levin and Daniel Robinson, "Rejoinder: Statistical Hypothesis Testing, Effect Size Estimation, and the Conclusion Coherence of Primary Research Studies," *Educational Researcher* 29, no. 1 (2000): 34–36.

About the Authors

Gene Pease is the cofounder and CEO of Capital Analytics, a consultancy revolutionizing the way companies evaluate their investments in people. With more than 25 years of experience as a CEO, and under his leadership, Capital Analytics has been recognized by Bersin and Associates (2012 Bersin Learning Leaders), *CLO Magazine* (Learning in Practice Awards in 2009, 2010, and 2011), Gartner (2009 and 2011 Hype Cycle for Human Capital Management "On the Rise Vendor" for Workforce Decision Support and 2008 Cool Vendor of the Year), and the ROI Institute (2011 First Place Recipient, Most Innovative Approach to ROI). Gene earned his MBA with honors in entrepreneur and venture management from the University of Southern California. He holds a BA in architecture from the University of Cincinnati. Gene currently holds a town council position in Chapel Hill, North Carolina.

■ ■ ■

Boyce Byerly, PhD, is the cofounder, chief scientist, and chief technical officer of Capital Analytics and has more than 20 years of experience designing and managing pure and applied research projects with high technology firms in the Research Triangle Area of North Carolina. He directed the Capital Analytics team that developed the methodology, software, and analytical tools that are the core intellectual assets of Capital Analytics. Boyce has published numerous articles and chapters on human capital analytics, knowledge representation, and computer-support cooperative work. Boyce earned his PhD from Duke University for interdisciplinary work in computer science and cognitive psychology, using advanced statistical techniques to investigate how the representation of information affects memory and problem solving. In addition, he holds an MS in computer science from Rutgers University and a

225

BS from Duke University, double-majoring in English and computer science and graduating cum laude. He is an active member of the International Society for Performance Improvement and is a professor at Bellevue University.

■ ■ ■

Jac Fitz-enz, PhD, is widely regarded as the father of human capital strategic analysis and measurement. He founded the famous Saratoga Institute and published the first HR metrics in 1978 and the first international HR benchmarks in 1985. *HR World* cited him as one of the top five "HR Management Gurus," IHRIM gave him its Chairman's Award for innovation, and SHRM chose him as one of the persons in the twentieth century who "significantly changed what HR does and how it does it." He has authored 12 books and more than 350 articles and has trained 90,000 managers in 46 countries on strategic management and measurement. His 2010 book, titled *The New HR Analytics*, introduced predictive analytics to human resources. Dr. Jac holds degrees from Notre Dame (BA), San Francisco State (MA), and University of Southern California (PhD) in organizational communications.

Index